MW00484429

Becoming
HOPE

BY HOPE GISELLE

CONTENTS

Print ISBN: 978-1-54394-066-4

eBook ISBN: 978-1-54394-067-1

DEDICATED TO:

Roosevelt Hadley I miss you more than I can ever say. You were the best grandfather I could ever ask for and you will NEVER BE REPLACED OR DUPLICATED. God outdid himself when he made you and put you in my life. You helped me stand as a man and respected my journey to becoming a woman. I love you so much and I know all of heaven is up there getting fat off of your cooking. Just save me a plate. So I can always say I'm coming home to a seat at the table of "the best in the bidness that ever did it H.A.D.L.E.Y" and don't you ever forget it!

Time is omnipresent, you'll never get away from is so make the best of what you have.

— Hope Giselle

PREFACE

I remember seeing the faces of the people in my community look at me in aww as I walked in my truth way before it became the trendy thing to do. I sacrificed my immediate comfort to prepare myself for the world around me and watched them pay off in small ways throughout my life's progression. After seeing Janet Mock and reading her story I formulated my own into words the world could understand and I thank her for being the face that helped me out of my proverbial closet. Her and women like her made this book possible, because they helped to make my thoughts more than distant dreams. I am a trans woman and I love that no matter the amount of fighting I have to do. It is my goal to stand , if for nothing else , myself.

"*I believe that telling our stories, first to our-selves and then to one another and the world, is a revolutionary act. It is an act that can be met with hostility, exclusion, and violence. It can also lead to love, understanding, transcendence, and community. I hope that my being real with you will help empower you to step into who you are and encourage you to share yourself with those around you.*"

— Janet Mock, Redefining Realness:
My Path to Womanhood, Identity,
Love & So Much More

CHAPTER 1

Slits in the closet

When I was a child, I devoted most of my time asking myself: why was I here? Where did I fit in? Did I belong, and could I have been dumped on the wrong planet by the Jesus bird on the way down? I had so many questions, but early on, I identified a couple things about myself I learned that if I was going to make it in this world, I would have to attain, absorb, and assimilate things that most five-year-old black boys from the projects wouldn't take up until that stereotypical white teacher at the local problem school made an attempt to "see something significant in them."

I didn't desire to be told I was exceptional. Hell, I was openly gay at five in the housing projects of Liberty City in Miami. I was the only person in my grade who could do a cartwheel and drop into a split with ease, and Moesha was my hero. Yes, the character from the hit TV sitcom starring "boy Is mine" singer Brandy was my hero. I regularly spoke to myself about what that meant, and what my story said about me to other people. How vital were their conclusions compared to my own? Was I really significant if only I knew it, and how did I alter that truth if it turned out to be accurate?

Growing up, the air was crisp, and time ran in slow motion. I was doing what felt comfortable, being who I was supposed to be at the time, which was fine by me because it proved to be easy. It took me forever to figure out relationships, and a lot of that had to do with the fact that most boys in my neighborhood weren't exploring sexuality like I was. I liked Barbies, playing with them in secret. I wanted to be on the cheer-leading team, and I loved Beyoncé.

It's safe to say that by ten I was a raging stereotype. Being gay did nothing but intensify my situation I had with bullies. I recall sitting in my room as a kid, not having cable, but finding a gay-centered show. The only catch was that it was entirely in Spanish. Although my Father's side of the family was from both Haiti and Cuba, I hadn't learned a lick of Spanish. This was largely due to my grandma on my father's side moving to New York for a large portion of my life. I guess in some ways that saved me. I could only imagine what some of those discussions would sound like in English if I had come out to her. I hold on to the memory of seeing two men kiss for the first time on TV. I found myself gasping for air while simultaneously resisting the strong impulse to be kissed that way. I wanted to be loved the way that Pedro seemed to love Juan, piecing together what I could through the lens of my ten-year-old mind and my lack of Spanish lessons. I wanted to feel feminine and soft. I wanted to feel like Juan.

I was in for a rude awakening though. There was this neighborhood bully when I was growing up. Unlike most of the others, he was special because he was handsome. I never discovered how old he was, but I knew he was older than me. I wanted to know which apartment he lived in, but I never found out. He was caramel-skinned and framed like a god of sorts. I noticed he was entirely black, but his eyes were a piercing blue-grey that practically always made me smile at the sight of them, and made just about everyone wonder where he came from. His teeth were perfect, and for a kid, he had this melodic deep voice that made him so much more attractive when he spoke!

One summer, I decided I would watch him and all the other "big boys" play basketball. I got my kicks out of watching them shirtless and sweaty, pretending to be drawing hopscotch squares with the girls. I kept my eyes on him at all times. I knew everything about his tendencies and his body. I learned when he would fake a shot or jump for the goal. My only curiosity was what was under the shorts: where did that tuft of hair on his stomach lead? I look back not knowing much about sex except what I had heard on the street and the things I could dream up while watching my gay tela-novela. I was innocent, but in just one very sudden experience, the bully was about to teach me a few things I needed to know about sexual experiences with men.

It was hot as hell and my grandma decided to force me outside to play. I figured if I had to, I'd make my way to the court where I could at least watch the boys play basketball. After making my way to the candy lady for a "froza cup" (a slang term for frozen juice in a cup: my flavor of choice being mango frozen), I headed to the empty court. I was pissed because it was hot and I made the walk, but no one was there. With my cup in hand cooling me off, I sat down and just watched the cars go by through the fence that surrounds the court. It was shaping up to be a peaceful day, until I got whacked with a basketball. I turned around to see it was Mr. Bully himself: shirtless, wearing his blue Nike gym shorts with the hole in the bottom right leg that he tore the day that one of the twins from across the street tripped him after they lost a pickup game. He looked down at me and asked, "you wanna play?"

I was in such shock that the words he was saying were actually aimed at me that I'm not really sure if I acknowledged the question. I just remember having no clue what I was doing. I was playing, he was letting me win, and I liked it. Then it started raining. We ran into this electrical closet that stank like piss and old cigars. It was pretty dark except for the slits of light coming from the closet like openings in the door. We didn't talk we just sat there waiting and looking and listening. Then he asked me the question, "you gay or somethin?" I just said "yea," hoping that the conversation would be over soon after. He stood up and my heart froze. He walked over to me and pulled his pants down. His dick was so big and veiny and hairy. I was instantly turned on, but being ten I had no idea what he wanted from me other than look at it. He pushed the head at my lips and said, "suck it." I looked at the door and took a nervous breath. He told me that he was "watching, there ain't nobody out there." Part of me was curious, while the other half of me was scared shitless. My mind was racing in fifty different directions. "Kiss me first," I said. "Kiss me and I'll do it." He pulled me up to him by my chin and leaned in to kiss me. I had never really kissed anyone before, let alone another boy, but his touch felt good.

He put my hand on his dick and it throbbed in my hand. He slowly pushed me down and I just did what felt natural. I had no clue if it felt good or if I was even sucking the right parts, but I knew I was enjoying the moment. He was keeping watch, so I let my guard down and he groaned out curse words while I explored. Then the door flew open. I tried to jerk away from him but he held my head tight. When I finally managed to snatch away, he came all over the wall. I was in tears and could barely breathe. I kept telling myself, "but he was watching! Why would he let them open the door?" In this case, "them" meant a dozen kids from the project complex just watching and laughing. He tucked his dick back in his blue shorts and t as he walked into the crowd of laughing kids, casually remarked, "told y'all he was a faggot."

The constant sense of depression and loneliness I felt once I hit puberty is largely due to that incident. It made me second guess sex. It wasn't fun. It was painful and embarrassing. I was waiting around for fairy tale love with boys that I didn't have any attachment to myself as a person. I wanted someone to choose me. I wanted to be held. I wanted to escape!

Around thirteen years old, I realized that my grandparents had a drug habit. They would take a walk every Friday, coming back to make my brother and I close the door. It would usually be an hour before my grandmother would come storming in with pupils as wide as the sun with her sights set on me. She always chose me! At first, it was mental abuse. She would make me clean the bathtub with a toothbrush and swear it wasn't clean each time. Every time I did it, I felt little pieces of me understanding those "white people shows." I understood the drama and the pain. I felt what they felt except for the fact that I wasn't white and my life wouldn't take a turn for the better. I couldn't expect my life to jump to my happy ending in the next 45 minutes, because it was just that: *Life*. It was real and I had to live through it, in it, and survive it if I was ever gonna be happy.

I recall smiling a lot, but never truly identifying as "happy." I chose to fake it. I was an actor, and this was my everyday role: a young, whimsical gay boy from the hood in Miami, Florida who just doesn't belong. I didn't have to audition for this part and it didn't pay, but I accepted it because if I didn't, I would be dead, or something in between life and death. I spent a lot of time in my head, replaying interviews with TV host about my latest film or book. I talked to myself a lot, because it was seldom that I found people that understood me. As social as I was, I was also very private about the things that bothered me the most. I was quiet about my anger, my dreams, and my ever changing discovery of love. I knew that it was unlikely that anyone would understand even if I did vent, so I tried not to.

I had one real friend as an adolescent: Jonathan. He was handsome and had the face of a full grown man at the age of seven and I remember the first day we met like it was yesterday because it was also my first brush with rejection. I walked into Ms. Sotolongo's class and sat down at a table by myself. I'm not sure if Jonathan was new to the school or just hadn't heard that I was the resident faggot yet, but he was about to find out. As a kid I hadn't learned modesty yet, and I was still hell-bent on normalizing these feelings that I felt naturally. He had this big head and these wide set jaws. He was wearing one of those noisy ass windbreakers and his feet where huge, but he was so handsome! I started vomiting words the second he sat down at the tiny little wooden desk next to me. I don't even remember thinking about the consequences. I turned to him and said, "hey can I tell you something?" He looked at me and with the biggest, grin he said, "what you gay huh?" I giggled in shock and fear and then reluctantly said, "yea, but don't tell anybody." He looked at me with the most confused look a kid that age could give and said, "don't you tell everybody anyway?"

We both laughed, and from that moment forward he was my best friend, my brother, and my first puppy love. He was the boy I knew my mom wished I could be. He had this fire about him that just screamed machismo and masculine. His aura was so full of life. He knew what he liked and stood firm in that. He had this unwavering hand about the things he believed and that's what made me love him. Jonathan made sure that if nothing else I remembered to stand up for myself. Like I said, it was that aura that attracted me to him. He wasn't the most popular boy among boys, but no-one ever really messed with him. They just knew better. Jay was always there for me whether I needed to talk, or cry, or someone to dance with. No matter how gay it might make him appear to the other boys, he always stood with me and choose to be as progressive as a young black man in the hood could be in 1999.

Most people wonder why I choose to make that a focus, or emphasis when talking about Jonathan. As I write this, I am reminding myself about the importance of the time and location of my story, and why this pivotal to the way things played out at that time in my life. I could have just conformed and fit into my environment, but instead I choose to embrace something far less comfortable which was ultimately being myself. As I speak about Jonathan and his influence on me to prove my manhood over my sexuality, I'm forced to remember the one time he wasn't there: the one time I had to stand up for myself and it scared me shitless.

In school, I was just as much of a target as I was at home. The only difference was the size and names of the bullies. At home it was blue shorts that made my first sexual experience a little less than enjoyable. In school, it was Dre and his stereotypically dumb and lanky sidekick, Johnny. Dre was short with a huge rock-shaped head and a crooked gap in his tooth, but he had the prettiest brown eyes you ever did see. He was stocky and built well for his age, probably from all the football he played. He was like a young Mr.T without the mohawk and way less money. On the other hand, Johnny was tall and skinny with the same crooked gap in his smile. It was probably their bonding agent. His clothes were always too big for him and he was the definition of a class clown. They hung out together mostly because they were both pretty behind when it came to school and comprehending work. I suppose they were stronger together than apart in that aspect. Dre was the brute and Johnny was the idol who pretty much lacked any real motivation of his own to do anything substantial.

It's important to understand that when I was in elementary school, my mom was typical hood rich. This meant we lived in the projects, but had every new shoe and outfit she could afford or get a booster to steal. I was well dressed and well kept. My hair was always cut low, I always had a lineup and, and I always smelled nice. All of this would've been alright if only it weren't coupled with the fact that I was somewhat of an unapologetic, raging queen at such a young age. I carried myself with confidence and allowed that confidence to be somewhat of an armor for me, a cloak of sorts. The only problem is that cloak didn't always hold and that armor wasn't always sturdy, especially against jealous bullies who weren't as fortunate as I was.

On this particular morning, I got to school after having a sip of my grandma's coffee. It was my little treat every now and then and I loved it. My grandma always had a way of making sure there was just the right amount of diabetes in that perfectly teddy bear colored mug to get me going. Then she'd bounce my ass right out of the door before my granddaddy could come downstairs and complain about it for the 600th time. Excited, I saw some girls jumping rope, and being me I jumped in. I was having a good time, minding my little gay-ass business until Johnny showed up. Dre was nowhere in sight, which made me happy and nervous at the same time.

He walked over to the rope and took it from the little girl with the giant pony tails and said, "let me try." Knowing he wasn't serious, the girl snatched the rope back while rolling her eyes, then waited with her end of the rope wrapped around her hands hoping he would just go. "Johnny why you even over here? Ain't no boys over here but you." I had obviously been clocked before I even knew I was trans, but we'll save that for later. Johnny looked over at me and said, "just 'cause he a fag-got don't mean he not a boy! If I gotta go, he gotta go too!"

He proceeded to grab my shirt and snatch me away from the area. By this point, there was a crowd of people. The laughs of eight kids felt like thirty. I snatched away from Johnny and pushed him so hard he fell and scuffed up his hands. That wasn't my intention, but by this point, my intention didn't matter. I had gotten myself into a fight and I had to finish it. My heart was racing. I remember the uncomfortable feeling of vomit coming from every part of my body. One of the girls I was jumping rope with took my backpack off to the side, and that made it official! Everyone knows that you never take off your backpack or put down your books in a setting like this. It was a signal to the opponent that you where indeed ready for a fight, and I hon-estly wasn't.

I had two and a half seconds to get ready. Just as I was gearing up to wear Johnny's skinny ass loose, Dre comes rumbling through the crowd, crooked tooth in tow. My heart stopped. I had a shot with Johnny, but Dre was gonna fuck me up and I knew it. All of my weight sank to my feet and I remem-ber Johnny getting up once he realized that Dre had entered to the circle of death: aka, the fight circle that would always form in a fight to ensure security can't get in too quick. Dre pushed

Johnny out of the way and quickly looked me in my eyes and said, "I can Beat this faggot."

I'm not sure why, but that word never sat well with me and touched more nerves than a Doctor did. Once I pinpointed his location, all I could see was Dre. I locked into him and beat him like he just told me that he would be the sole reason for Beyoncé's death in 2065. I kept telling myself, "hit him so he can't hit you! Hurt him so that he can't hurt you!" I punched him in the face until security came and snatched me away. I didn't stop partially because I knew if I did, he'd kick my ass, but also because I was enjoying it! I enjoyed projecting my anger on him in the form of an ass whooping. I liked how it felt when he started to bleed, and the crowd made it more embarrassing for him to be in the situation. When I got pulled off, I can only recall not being done and the instant fear that I was now going home to face the music from my mom for the first time ever. I was in trouble and I knew it. I was getting suspended. That was beyond a shadow of a doubt.

I sat in the office crying. Even after being victorious, I kept telling myself that it wasn't me, that I wasn't capable of being that mean or hurting someone the way I just did. I came up with all the excuses for my inexcusable behavior. I thought about why I had let myself become a catalyst for the ignorance that I hated being inflicted upon me. One of the neighborhood moms saw me sitting there with tears in my eyes and asked me what happened. I told her, and she assured me she'd talk to my mom and let her know that the fight wasn't my fault. The sentiment was nice, but if you knew my mother, you would know why that "promise" was anything but solid in my book. I was still scared shitless, and time was not on my side for what appeared to be the first time that day. Usually, I'd have to wait what seemed like years for the final bell to chime, but that day went by as fast as an instagram challenge. I walked as slow as I could down the street, through the basketball court and to my house with my referral and suspension paper in hand. As always, I could see my grandmother waiting on me through the window. Before I could even reach the handle, my grandfather swung the screen door open and they both had that "you bout to getcho ass whooped" face on.

My mom was the main disciplinarian while my grand-parents just handed out the necessary spankings and deadly pinches. I set the papers on the table and immediately that moment my grandma picked them up, reading the word *suspension* with the most surprised face I think I'd ever seen her have at the time. We all broke neck at the sight of my moms car booming into the parking lot and up to her usual space (which hadn't been marked, but was definitely hers). I think I success-fully gulped for the first time. My head started to hurt and sud-denly I couldn't breathe all at once. My grandmother stood up and almost pushed me out of the way to tell my mama the news. "You know this boy done been suspended?"

It was over. I just prepared for the worst, and then the most beautiful thing happened. She walked past my grandma, sat at the table and said, " mama I know. He got in a fight." My grandma went from pissed and confused, to just plain hysteri-cal. "A fight? With who? My grand baby don't bother nobody! We going down to that school tomorrow!" My mama just rolled her eyes, then looked at me and asked, "why were you fight-ing?" I told her how Dre and Johnny had been bothering me the whole time, always called me a faggot or a sissy, and about how Johnny snatched me by my shirt. Instead of the sympathy that I saw on TV during these situations, my mom made it my fault. She told me if I didn't act like one, I wouldn't have been in a fight. She looked me square in the face and asked me, "you think you a girl?" I said no. She asked again. "You sure?" I nod-ded my head. "Yes" I said. "Oh ok, cause imma tell you this: the day you think you gone be anything other than my son is the day I don't know you no more. Do you understand me?" She said that with the conviction of God himself in her voice. Although I had no clue that I even had the choice to be anything but her son, I knew I didn't want to find out and test the waters either. I wiped my face with the back of my hand and she said to me, "I'm not gone beat you for fighting and protecting yourself, but you better stop whatever you doing to make them pick on you." I nodded my head yes. I started to walk towards the stairs when I heard a voice say, "aye , did you win?"

CHAPTER 2

Love and Basketball

My life was full of lessons. Most of the time, unbeknownst to me, the lessons would change depending on the choices that I made. I created spaces for myself as I got older that led me down paths that either put me in really great positions, or left me feeling dank and stupid. One of the early lessons I learned was that love didn't have a gender. I knew early on that I wasn't attracted to girls, or so I thought. I could acknowledge the beauty of women and admire them, but the idea of courting and actually enjoying sexual pleasure from a woman was a dream deferred. I saw women as these regal creatures to not be tampered with. I had strong women in my family and modeled myself after strong female characters from TV shows and books I had read over the course of my short life. I admired the Greek goddesses, and if I'm being honest, I had a bad taste in my mouth for most men, especially black ones. Black men made me feel embarrassed of who I was. They judged me, my preferences, the way I walked, and even my values. Men were the enemy until proven innocent, which I guess explains why I tended to fall in love with every man that was nice to me at that age.

But then there was Kayshelia: a little light skin girl with a raspy voice, long sandy brown hair and a gap that only a grade school kid and mom could appreciate. Although she grew to be my first and only female love and girlfriend, that road wasn't all roses and daisies. I'll never forget how I met her. Johnathan and I were on the court as usual one morning, waiting for our teachers to pick us up. As was typical, Jonathan felt the need to teach me how to do some boyish thing. He never really tried to change me, but he always wanted to equip me with the tools to be ready in case other guys wanted to try and embarrass me and he wasn't around. We did karate together and he taught me basic football moves so I wouldn't get tackled.

On this particular morning, I was getting a basketball lesson. For a big-headed ten year old, Jay had a lot of control over the ball. His hands were big and his aim was amazing. He was trying to teach me how to do a free-throw from the three point line. He gave me all the tools and set up the shot for me. At the time, I convinced myself that I was Michael Jordan and I just knew I couldn't fail. I tossed the ball and it bounced off the backboard to the right of the hoop, smacking Kaysheila dead in the forehead. The way it bounced off of her was ridiculously funny, so Johnathan and I both gave out the typical "ooooh shit," and then burst into laughter. Apparently Kayshelia didn't find it as humorous as we did. In fact, she didn't think it was funny at all. She was pretty pissed.

I ran over to her to apologize the situation away, but it was too late. Before I could get two words out, she was calling me everything but a child of god. For a ten year old, the girl had a vocabulary of curse words like no other. I had to retaliate so I told her she was a big headed bitch. Then she told me I was ugly and I better get outta her face before she called her auntie. I then proceeded to tell her to go and get her fat auntie not knowing she was just two feet away watching the whole exchange play out. Kayshelia walked over to the gate where her aunt was watching. To my surprise, she hadn't moved from her spot, although we were clearly arguing. I followed because I was a child and wanted to plead my case too. Why should I let her tell the whole story when I knew she would lie? We both got to her aunt at about the same time. Before I could open my mouth she was pointing in my direction, swinging the long sandy brown ponytail she had placed perfectly on the top of her head back and forth, yelling about how I called her a bitch with a big head. I cut her off in the effort to prove my innocence, and then it was just one big jumbled mess of two kids rambling on and on with no real end in sight.

Her aunt had finally had enough and told us both to settle down and stop all that fighting. She told me that I was handsome and told Kay that she needed to be more ladylike instead. I guess you can say that was my first taste of both male privilege and misogyny all wrapped into one. I have to admit, although I didn't identify as a man, those perks felt good right away. I got a pass simply for being a handsome boy and she still got reprimanded even though I called her bighead! It was kinda great, especially because I felt like she had really jumped the gun on the whole situation in the first place. It was all a mistake and had she let me explain it would've all been fine.

What I did notice though was the fact that, for the first time in my life, I very faintly saw her beauty as something that needed to be acted upon, and what was even more shocking to me was that I did! Kay and I had the same class and as the days went by I had plenty of talks with myself about how to go about this. I was gay and everyone knew it, but here I was trying to talk to one of the prettiest girls in school, mostly because she fit that light skin, long hair look that most of the girls in school deemed popular had. Yet, my attraction came from a different place. I really liked her for no other reason than the fact that she existed and liked knowing that she was in the world. I didn't really know how to go about it, so I sought the help of my best friend Johnathan, who was simply happy that I even found the strength to admit that I liked an actual girl. Keep in mind that it was about 1998, or something like that, and men's approach to women was so flawed, especially on a grade school level.

"Write her a note," he said. "Just ask her if she thinks you're cute, and if she says yes, then ask her of she wanna be your girl. And if she says yes to that, then ask her to let you hunch." Now, for those of you that are unfamiliar with the term, "hunching" was basically dry humping and what we intercity kids in Miami thought sex was at the time. You would kiss, touch, and then grind on each other till you're tired, since ejaculation wasn't really a thought or option at that age. Considering the fact that my attraction to girls was in its entirety new, the thought of hunching just seemed like a bit much, but Jonathan had more experience with girls, so I let him be my Master Splinter and teach me the way of the men that play.

After talking to Jay, I walked into Mrs. Ramsey's class with a new outlook on life and women. Kayshelia was gonna be my girlfriend. I had done the work, I had logged the man hours, and she was gonna be my new girl. Well, my only girl. The fact of the matter was that she just had something different about her. It was something special and I couldn't put my finger on what it may have been. Kay was beautiful and her smile was golden, but so was Bianca's or Diona's. What about this girl made me feel the butterflies that up until that point I'd only gotten from men? That's a question that I've still yet to answer, but I'm forever grateful that I didn't reject the feelings I had for her.

It was a Wednesday, and I remember because I planned it out that way. I put on my extra strong cologne, my gray hush puppies with my corduroy overalls, and my Tommy shirt. I felt good about the journey I was about to embark on. I walked to school with a little extra pep in my step that day, almost skipping. I felt dopey, and halfway through my stride I realized I must have looked like an idiot and kinda slowed down. When I got to the cafeteria, I looked up and down for Johnathan. As usual, I found him, and we went over my plan once again. I would pass the note, get the response, and then boom! She would be my girlfriend and we would be "hunching" like normal little elementary school kids do. It was fool proof and I was gonna make sure it went off without a hitch.

Mrs. Ramsey came to get us from the pick up area, and Kayshelia was in line at the very front like a typical miss goodie two shoes. When we got to class, we all pulled out our homework and Mrs. Ramsey came around to collect it. Although we had to look at her everyday today she looked...different. She looked at me in a new way. It was almost as if she knew I had plans on being a dirty little scumbag boy that day and wanted to catch me in the act. When we caught each other's gaze, I stood my ground. The mole above her lip seemed to reposition itself just to tell me to *Fuck off*, but I was persistent. I held my homework up and that day I won my first student-teacher stare down! I felt triumphant to say the least.

After we got our books out for social studies, I made my move on Kay as planned. I wrote a note that simply said, "do you think I'm cute, yes or no?" I passed it. A few seconds later, I got it back with the yes circled! I felt like the man. With my new found confidence, I went on to the next phase of the plan. I passed yet another note where I wrote, "do you wanna be my girlfriend?" To my surprise this note came back with a positive yes too. I was in the clear and it was my time to seal this deal. With Jonathan's thumbs up of approval I was all in. My last note simply simply said, "can I see your coochie?" This time it wasn't passed right back. Instead, Kay raised her hand, waved Mrs. Ramsey over and passed the note to her. I was embarrassed, and although I didn't know much about sexual respect for women at the time, I knew I had royalty screwed up. Kay looked pissed, Ramsey looked shocked and disgusted, and the rest of the class just wanted to know what the note said.

I sat there sitting on my hands until it was time to go to lunch. I knew I had to apologize and I wanted to make it snappy before Kay didn't wanna be my girlfriend anymore. After we made it to the cafeteria, I found Kay and asked her to follow me to the water fountain on the inside of the school building. It didn't dawn on me until now how poorly lit the hallway was. It gave me serial killer movie vibes with the door closed, but it made for the perfect mood setter in my ten year old brain. Kay got to the water fountain, adjusted her sandy brown ponytail, and pursed her lips avidly before giving me the most attitudinal "whatchu want?" in the world. I liked her so much for no reason at all, and that was part of the reason why. She was bold, but so sweet when unprovoked to be a stone cold bitch and it really helped that I thought she looked a lot like Beyoncé, She always disagreed, but that was definitely a part of why I had such an affinity for her. I took a deep breath and let my apology go like I was trying to avoid a lifetime jail sentence. I'm realizing now that for such young kids, we had a really honest conversation about boundaries and feelings. When it was all said and done, I had a girlfriend and that meant more to me than life itself at the time.

I reveled in having a girlfriend. I had no clue what I was doing, but Kay had a schedule that I soon committed to memory. I would meet her at her house some mornings to walk her to school. I would sit in the waiting area with her. I would eat lunch with her unless I pissed her off. Then I had to sit with Jonathan. Last but not least, I liked walking her home from school. Even if that meant I was late getting home myself, it was worth it! The puppy love was real and I was in it deep. Although I still had very strong attractions for men, Kay just made my body do something different. And our first kiss felt like magic because of that.

It was a rainy day after school. Kay's mom drove the public transit buses, so she had to stay in the after care program. I often skipped my after school tutoring session to be with her. We sat on the playground for a while and talked, made fun of each other, mimicked things we had seen on TV and it wasn't long before we were back at our water fountain. Once again she was adjusting her ponytail and I just watched her. It had been about a month, but in preteen time that was a lifetime of courtship. Once she got her drink from the fountain my private thoughts crept up from my stomach through my throat and out of my mouth. In a fit of verbal diarrhea, I asked if I could kiss her. To my surprise she said yes. I proceeded to process every TV show, movie, and even real life heterosexual kiss I'd ever seen and turned it into one bomb-ass SpiderMan, Romeo & Juliet,

Cinderella-and-the-princes-wedding moment. I did everything right and I could tell she liked it and I loved it.

That night, we talked on the phone until my grandma forced me off. Because I had spent all night going over the details with Kay, I spent all morning filling in Johnathan about the kiss and how it all went down. We were sitting on the playground, waiting on Mrs. Ramsay, as usual. In the middle of the conversation, Johnathan gets this weird look in his eyes and starts to look right past me. Not sure of himself, he asked, "Yo is that Kayshelia?" He then said "Man I think her and Gregneisha about to fight." I sprung up and ran across the court to see that Jonathan was right. I had no idea what the fight was about, but I knew I had some civic duty to be in the area as it took place.

They argued for a little bit until I saw Mrs. Ramsey coming up from the main building and grabbed Kays arm. Gregneisha who never seemed to have problem with me before was beyond upset. Between you and me, I was doing her a favor. Kay was known for kicking ass and I honestly don't think it would've been pretty if I had let her get a hold of her. She looked Kay square in the face, in front of the newly formed crowd and said, "that's why yo boyfriend a faggot." I was immediately embarrassed for her, because while we were dating and I liked Kayshelia a lot, I knew I still liked boys too, but what Kay said next will live with me forever. She didn't look awkward or embarrassed at all. She grabbed her book bag out of my hand, took me by the other one and said, "well if he's a faggot, then he's my faggot." I didn't realize it at the time, but that was an epic read and the crowd went wild for it. I thought about it a lot and that was the moment I fell in love with that girl and I've loved her ever since.

CHAPTER 3
Turing Point

At some point around the time I turned thirteen, I realized that life wasn't the easiest thing on Earth. Grades got harder to maintain, and I was starting to find my individuality, which meant that my environment didn't often lend itself to my dreams. In the hood, you had plenty of people telling you to get out, making sure that you knew it was possible, all while staying stagnant themselves. This dynamic confused me, especially when I saw the potential in people. While I tended stick to myself, I would watch as the the older boys would gravitate towards the guys that sat on crates outside the Arab stores, shooting dice. Trying to mingle with the girls in my neighborhood always got me in some sort of trouble; not to mention that our interests were usually just as different as the boys were. I was awkwardly aware of the fact that I was only popular because of my ability to be unapologetically different, and by different I mean gay. Most of the kids I grew up with that I knew personally would hold fast to the the promise land of denial in exchange for a taunt-free life.

Myself on the other hand? I'd like to think that if I did a make a "choice," then my choice was to live out loud and understand that I made people uncomfortable with my truth, which was their problem not mine. This early reality became a mantra of sorts for me as I pushed through middle school. It was always evident to me that I never wanted to live in Miami forever. While the beaches were nice, the weather always seemed to be just right, and celebrities frequented our slice of the peninsula. I wanted more than South Beach, Liberty City, and Aventura. I wanted art and culture. So, I lived in a place in my head that was perfect so long as no one else knew about it.

In middle school, I was a little bit afraid to be exactly who I was. Everything seemed to be so easy, but at the same time it confused me. I had some of the same friends from elementary school, due in large part to the fact that the buildings were connected. So most kids just transferred right over and the new people had to fall in line, but for the most part the cafeteria was the same, the uniforms were the same, and I had to deal with the same people, which usually meant the same bullies. Or at least people trying to bully me. I remember feeling like I was flying under the radar. I had made it all the way to my eighth grade year without a single issue. I felt like I was going to finally get out of school without a hitch.

By this point, I had been to two separate middle schools and had gotten kicked out of both. One of them was because I had allowed myself to fall victim to the woes of trying to be a cool kid. In short, let's just say it's never cool to take body shots of chocolate syrup leftover from the ice cream social off of your classmate in the middle of a school lesson. I got kicked out of the other one simply because I got into fight after fight and the principal finally had enough of me. So I ended up in the one middle school that I absolutely didn't want to go to: Charles R. Drew Middle School. It lived in the heart of the old project complexes that I had thought I finally escaped by the time I reached my teens. My mom had finally taken us back from my grandmother, and we moved into her nice house that was at least seven or eight blocks away. That doesn't seem far, but for me it felt like it was a whole new city.

On my first day of school, I remember lacing up these tan and white Jordans. I was nowhere near a sneaker fanatic, but my mom and stepdad were, and they told me that they were the new shoes that everybody would be wearing, and let me tell you everybody was wearing them. I walked up to the old creaky gates in front of the school only to be met by thirty other kids (and that's no exaggeration) who were wearing the same exact shoes as me. For the first time, I felt my soul leave its body and beg for its individuality back. We were all wearing the same Walmart cargo shorts and either a gold, burgundy, or white shirt. I felt like I was in the Twilight Zone. The only thing different had to be the hairstyles and the haircuts, but we all looked like carbon copies. We were almost like a black ghetto version of the Stepford wives, except I wasn't Nicole Kidman, and these kids were definitely not paid actors. But, I had to make the best of the situation. I remember for months going about my business just waiting to graduate. Not wanting to be seen or heard: just wanting to get out.

I almost made it until I got in trouble and landed myself in CSI. If you're not familiar with what that is, just think prison for your kids in school without kicking them out of school. It wasn't necessarily better than hell, but it was better than actual suspension. On this one particular day, I decided I just had to be late to school because I was going to get a honey bun. The only problem was the only machine that had them was five miles across campus, but I was determined. I got my honey bun, but I also got caught in the CSI sweep for the morning. I landed in there with a bunch of the other delinquents. Some of them were my friends, some of them were strangers, and some of them were people I wish I didn't know. The only good part about CSI was that it was run by the most beautiful, bald headed black man that you ever did see. Mister Harding had to be at least 6'4", with caramel skin, and he always wore collared shirts that were just a little too tight, but with a body like his, nobody seemed to care. All the girls and I agreed that if we had to see him in CIS everyday... I'd get caught getting honey buns everyday.

I passed the time in CSI by writing dirty stories. I had stumbled upon some erotica books that my grandmother kept under her bed. I guess you could say that was the start of me trying to be an author. The stories always intrigued me, but in the back of my mind, I knew I could write something better. Something with more spunk . Something that would make me hornier than the washed down Cinemax crap that I was reading. I used one of my spiral notebooks that my mom had clearly bought for schooling and turned it into one of the best middle school erotica's that you ever did read. I passed it to Kay, she read it and then passed it to a bunch of her friends. Before I knew it, I had people asking me to add onto the story, and everything was fine until Mr. Harding got his hands on it. He barely got through the first page before he was looking at me like I had slapped his mother at Sunday school. He gave me one of the dirtiest looks he could possible give and then politely told me in front of the entire room that I would be spending the rest of the week in CSI. Of course, everybody found it hilarious, but to my surprise everybody who laughed got an extra day of CSI. I laughed silently because I didn't want to get an extra week on top of the one I had just acquired.

At lunchtime, the kids who were in CSI had to sit at separate lunch tables, and after everyone finished eating we had to help the cafeteria ladies pick up plates, sweep the floors, and wipe the tables. I got stuck on table duty with a guy we all knew as Shanebang. Shane was fat, ridiculously dark, had unkempt hair way before it became a trend in black culture and a horrible attitude. Honestly, I believe he went on to play the main character in one of the Planet of the Apes movies, but I can't prove that so don't hold me to it. In the middle of us wiping the tables down, while I was wishing I was Beyoncé yet again, Shane hisses at me. You know the hiss, that stupid thing that all guys do when they are catcalling but don't want people to know they are actually talking to you. That snake-like sound that annoys every woman, and even though I wasn't identifying as one, it annoyed me. I looked over in his direction and tried to muster up all the attitude I could find in my body before I simply blurted, "What!?"

Shane looked around and then motioned with his finger for me to come over closer. I reluctantly walked over, threw my rag on the table, and asked him what it was that he wanted. He was speaking in a hushed tone. I could barely hear what he was saying. Finally, after I had enough trying to play Inspector Gadget, I just asked him what he wanted. To my surprise, he was asking if I could give him head after school. I was pissed. I didn't really know how to react and so I did the first thing that came to mind... I went the fuck off. It's all a blur at this point, but I do know I called his mom several types of reptiles and three different types of prostitutes. Just when he was about to retaliate, Mister Harding came to the cafeteria to pick us up, but that didn't stop him from reminding me that after school, I would have to answer to him for the things that I had just said. I don't remember being afraid, I just remember thinking that I shouldn't have to fight when he was the one that did something wrong. The sad part about it was that I knew no one would believe the gay kid.

Once we got back into the CSI room, it seemed like time ran slow. Shane and his goons kept looking at me and making the most stupid faces while everybody else whispered about the reason we would be fighting. I just sat in the back of the classroom and kept writing in my little notebook. This time, it was a journal. I just remember writing my thoughts about why I was gonna be fighting him and why he felt it was okay to ask me to suck his dick even though he didn't like me. I asked myself all types of questions, mostly about whether or not this was all I was good for since I was gay.

Just as I got into the swing of my journal, the time that had been moving slowly kicked into hyper drive. Before I knew it, it was 3 o' clock. My palms started sweating and I got those butterflies you get right before the roller coaster takes the big dip, but I refused to look like a punk. I grabbed my bag and walked out of the school as usual. As I made my way down the stairs, all of my friends who had heard about the fight followed me out. There was Brittney, Kay, Kiara, Jasmine and Jo-Jo. I felt a little better knowing that I at least had some sort of support, but what nobody counted on was another fight happening. Before Shane could actually approach me, two random girls started pulling at each others' weave in the middle of the street. So of course like the middle school children we were, we all made the fight circle, gathering around them while we pulled out our 2004 cell phones and recorded, cheering for our victor. It was almost like a form of ratchet Roman Colosseum fighting, except no death was necessary. So long as somebody started bleeding, the other person was announced the winner.

I almost forgot that I had my own problems in the midst of watching everything go down. After the girls broke themselves up, I looked across the crowd only to see that Shane was still determined on picking his own fight with me. A random guy came over to me and told me to meet them at the end of the block. It was only a couple feet away, but it felt like I was walking a plank and I knew I was about to be pushed over. Brittney and Jo-Jo both urged me to take a different way home. Apparently, Shane had no intentions on fighting me alone and had invited his cousins from the high school nearby to have a piece of the pie. The only problem was, I was more afraid of my mother kicking my ass than I was of these guys, and because of the little fight between those girls, I was already late getting home. There was no way I could take a different way. I had to either go through those guys or explain to my mother what had happened, and without a fight, she was not going to have any sympathy for me. At least this way, I could say that I got jumped.

With a bunch of people behind me, all of whom were surprised that I was still walking in the direction of the obvious mob of high-schoolers determined to kick my ass, I pushed towards the corner. Without hesitation, I ran towards Shane, grabbing a hold of him and anybody else that came within arms reach, and started swinging for my life. That didn't last long. I'm not exactly sure how many guys were there or how many jumped in for the sake of beating up on me because I was who I was. All I knew is that it was definitely the most feet and hands I had ever seen in my life. They had me pinned down with my shirt over my head, punching and kicking me, and of course calling me the usual faggot every now and then. Eventually, the only thing that got them off of me were my friends. I couldn't see them but I could hear Brittney, Jo-Jo, Kiara and Jasmine all yelling at them to stop.

Then the police sirens started. I don't think I've ever been so happy to hear sirens in my life. The guys all peeled off one by one and I was finally able to stand up. Even though there had to be at least twenty people beating up on me at the same time, I didn't have a single scratch, bruise, bump or lump. And most importantly, I wasn't bleeding. I gathered myself together and started to walk home like normal. I made my way down the street, but as I passed the Arab store, I saw my grandmother walking towards me. I almost peed on myself until I realized my mom wasn't far behind her. Apparently, word got out that I was being jumped and it wasn't long before my entire family showed up like the black mafia.

At that point, it was too late. All the guys involved had either run home or to some hideaway spot. And even if I did see who was beating on me, I didn't hang out with the boys anyway, so they would have been impossible to name. The only person that I knew for sure deserved any of my attention was Shanebang. My mom was furious. All she kept asking was who did this to me and the only person I could name out of the twenty people was him, but she couldn't do much. She gave me one simple instruction: wherever I saw him, no matter who was around, no matter what time of day, whenever he came into my view, I was to fuck him up, no excuses.

I took those instructions literally. I slept on those words, then woke up and went to school with them, because I had gotten an extra week of CSI due to my erotica fiasco, I reported straight there. As soon as I opened the door to the dungeon-like classroom they kept us in, there he was. Mister Bang was wearing the same uniform from the day before with the same unkempt hair and the same dirty Timberland boots. Without hesitation, with my mother's words echoing in the back of my mind, I took off my backpack and beat the shit out of Shane. I wasn't a fighter, but I have to tell you it felt good. The way that everybody cheered me on. The surprised look on Mister Harding's face. The way that the rest of the guys looked at me hoping that they wouldn't be next. It all felt so good, and I reveled in the feelings that I had in that moment.

Mister Harding finally got me off of him and drug me to the front office. He had apparently heard about the fight already from the day before and gave me a silent gaze of approval for standing up for myself. It wasn't long before my mom got to the school. Now like I said, I wasn't a fighter, and I definitely wasn't somebody that got in trouble often, so whenever I had to make a trip to the office, even if it was for defending myself, I was nervous. My mom stood next to me, silently, until the principal finally made time to call us into the office. She sat there with the most disgusted look on her face as if I was a regular in her office. She almost started to paint me as the stereotypical problem child, one of the many that we had at our school. Until my mom stopped her dead in her tracks and filled her in on everything that had happened. She changed her tune really quick after that and just gave me a slap on the wrist. I remember having to spend the rest of the week with Mister Harding as his personal assistant of sorts while Shane was sent home on regular suspension. I've gotta tell you that had to be the best week of my life; especially considering that Mr. Harding seemed to be working out a lot that week.

I managed to make it through the rest of the year with little to no issues. I even found a new teacher who would let me hide out in his classroom and do hoodrat things with my friends. Mister Palmer was this overweight but super sweet teddy bear of a man. He was one of those teachers that everybody seemed to run over because he was too nice, and honestly, too big to chase you. He was my reason for loving the musical Chicago and his classroom was the first place that I had ever heard the music from the film. He explained to me the premise of the story and gave me his synopsis on all of his favorite characters. While he didn't smell good, he had a heart of gold. I just wished he would have shaved more often. Mister Palmer was obviously lonely, and even more obviously gay, but with the vain rules of the gay community, there was no way he was going to find anybody to settle down with at his weight. So I believe he just settled for being really nice to his students so that he would have people to talk to and I had no problem being his friend. We talked about everything from theater, to museums, to art, and even music. He introduced me to jazz, and told me a lot about African culture. I even turned him on to the pussycat dolls. Our friendship was an even exchange. Or, at least as even as it could be for a thirteen year old and their social studies teacher.

Then, he did the unthinkable. If you know me, and I mean really know me, you know that I am a part of the Beyhive and I love Beyoncé almost as much as I love breathing. But in my thirteen years of life, I had never seen her perform. One day before school ended, I got word from one of my friends that Mister Palmer wanted to see me as soon as school let out. When the bell rang, I walked over to his classroom and poked my head in. My friend Bianca was there with her boyfriend who just so happened to be Mister Palmer's godson. They were sitting in a corner making out while Palmer pretended to be oblivious to the situation and so did I. I walked over to his desk, and once I was within sniffing distance, I was hit with his aroma which reminded me of pee and hospital. But once I saw his smile, I got over myself, as usual. He had this look about him that day, and I couldn't quite put my finger on it. I wasn't sure whether I should be creeped out or happy that he looked so happy. He took an envelope out of his satchel placed it on the desk and said, "That's for you."

I looked at him in confusion and then I realized that Bianca and her boyfriend had stopped making out and they both had the same look Mister Palmer had before he pulled the envelope out: giddy and stupid. I looked at all of them in confusion, then ripped the envelope open. There were two thin slices of paper in it, and upon reading them and realizing that I was holding two tickets with fantastic seats to the Beyoncé experience, I lost my entire mind! I ran around the classroom for what had to be at least five minutes, rolling on the floor, and doing a cartwheel before giving Mister Palmer the biggest hug I could give any-one, despite his smell. Apparently, Bianca and her boyfriend had already known and they were just as excited as I was. After asking him if they were real and they were for me at least a thou-sand times, I grabbed the tickets, putting them in my book-bag before floating home singing "Crazy in Love" along the way.

I got home, and with all of the excitement that I could muster, I ran into my mom's room and presented her with my golden tickets to see Queen Bey. She was excited and confused, excited because she knew I loved her and confused because she was trying to figure out why my social studies teacher had gifted me tickets that were worth at least $600 a piece. I saw her wanting to kill my joy and then choosing not to. The concert was a week away, and because my mother was my mother, all she could think about was what I was going to wear. That week seemed to fly by. I listened to my Beyoncé CD more than I had ever listened to it in my life. I watched the concerts back to back and practiced every dance move. You would have thought that I was going to be sitting in the front row, but I just wanted to be ready. My mom and I picked out this really cool jean and shirt set. It had patchwork pockets and baby blue detailing. It was the beginning of my gay wardrobe, mostly because it actually fit, unlike everything else in my closet.

The day of the show we got ready and drove at least 45 minutes away. My mom reluctantly paid $20 for parking and $18 for us to get drinks, which is something she'd never let me for-get. We got to our seats which were really awesome and sat through performances by Robin Thicke and Sara Bareilles, which led to me consequently falling in love with their music too. Then, the lights went off and the crowd went crazy. This was my first concert so I didn't really know the etiquette. It wasn't until I saw my first firework flash that I knew she was making an entrance. I was in the same space as Beyoncé for the first time in my life, and I completely lost my mind. I don't think I sat down for the entire two hours that we were there. I sang every song loudly and danced so hard that I started to sweat. The people behind us looked at my mom in shock and all she could keep saying was, "He loves this lady," with a smile on her face. I remember for the first time feeling like she wasn't embarrassed of me even though this was one of those rare times where my gay flag was flying so high that I might as well have been an episode of "Queer as Folk."

That was my first time seeing Beyoncé live and all it did was remind me of why I love her. It was inspiring and beautiful and I was never one to pass out or cry but for the first time I knew why people did. I understood why people would look ridiculous in the videos. The lady was iconic and the feeling I felt in that room is still unmatched. We got home that night and even my mother who claims that she doesn't like Beyoncé could not shut up about it. It was a great way to end my middle school career, even though afterwards my mother made me stop talking to Mister Palmer. She said that my stepfather had told her that it made him uncomfortable, and she agreed. In the back of my mind, so did I, but I felt bad because I knew that I was one of the only people that he felt like he could communicate with without being ridiculed behind his back. Even though he had his flaws, I never openly spoke about them with anybody and I knew he appreciated that. I did break the rules on the day of graduation though. Before I left, I had to give him one last bear hug for the road and thank him for introducing me to Chicago and making middle school a little less of a hellhole.

CHAPTER 4

Deja Vu

f I could give my younger self any advice, it would be to stay
in the closet with my family longer. I had never been afraid to
be who I was, the only problem I had was telling my mom who
I was. Opening up to her about my sexuality was always a task
I was never ready to complete. Nothing that she could say, do,
or hint at made it any easier. Over the years, she had more than
enough reasonable doubt. She had found letters, porn cut outs,
books, and even heard things from other people. Still, I never
verbally said anything until I got in trouble.

This one particular day I was at my grandmother's house.
School was sucky. I had been slapped in the face by a guy who
I didn't know because of something that I admitted to a girl that
I thought I could trust. To hold onto his masculinity, he embarrassed me. When I got home, all I wanted to do was get my
homework out of the way, take a nice hot shower, and watch
TV. After I had everything done and finally had a chance to sit
down, I turned the TV on to MTV. This was back when TRL was
still a thing, and just as I was changing the channel, the DeJa Vu
video by Beyoncé came on. This was my anthem at the time and
like most things queen Bey related I knew every move. I was in
the room having a complete and utter outer body experience.
I had pictured myself in the middle of nowhere in a grass skirt

with perfectly curled hair and beautifully bronze skin dancing in the dirt for my husband.

Then, my fantasy was ruined. My grandmother had always been in support of my dancing and all of my other effeminate tendencies, but for some reason, on this day, she felt the need to criticize me. She walked past the room and with the ugliest tone said to me, "Stop that faggot shit," and then insinuated that my dancing was the reason for me being picked on and beat up. I had never really had the courage to stand up to my grandmother, but that day I couldn't take it and I responded back before I could even think about the words that I was going to use. Before I knew it, I was outside on the front porch crying while my grandmother was calling my mom. My grandfather who seemed to be the great white hope understood exactly where I was coming from and couldn't understand for the life of him why I was getting in trouble for dancing. It all happened so fast. As I was sitting on the porch waiting for my mom to get there, I realized that I was in so much trouble for simply being who I was. For the first time, as I waited on what was sure to be a decent ass whooping, I wasn't afraid of my mother. I was upset with the idea that I couldn't be who I truly was around my mother. My grandfather was upset about the entire thing and decided to take a walk. That was his way of coping so that he didn't have to be around when I got what he thought was an unfair punishment.

Shortly after he told me he loved me and left me on the front porch, my mother's white car came zooming up to the front of the house, and she jumped out with her belt and an attitude. She banged on the door for my grandmother to let her in. Before I could get into the house well enough, I could feel the sting of the ragged leather on my back as she cursed at me incoherently for about five minutes. At some point, my grandmother asked her to take it to the room so that she didn't have to watch. She dragged me by my shirt back into the room and made my little brother go to the living room. She slammed the door and then proceeded to ask me what my problem was and why I felt the need to disrespect my grandmother. All I could do was cry. I knew at this point I had to say something more than *I don't know*. I knew I had to be honest, but being honest in this situation meant coming out. I could barely feel my fingers, and I started to shake as I explained why we had gotten into it in the first place. I remember my mom sitting down slowly relinquishing the floor to me and actually listening. At this point, now that the belt was out of swing position, I felt a little bit safer to speak. I remember recounting the story and visually seeing her nod her head in agreement with me. It felt good to feel like I was finally being heard, but then it was time. I had to actually say it. I had to tell my mom that I was gay. I blinked my eyes and swallowed my own spit more times than I can actually remember. My throat was dry, my back was sweaty and my voice cracked every time I tried to say it.

Finally, my mom grew annoyed, picked up the belt, flung it over her shoulder and with anger in her voice she said, "Say it." I'm not sure if it was the belt or the intimidation tactic, but the words flew out of my mouth. The only thing that I could say was, "I'm gay." I remember having a moment with myself right after the words flew out and standing there in complete shock as all of the little versions of me in my head went into malfunction overdrive. If I were a cartoon, that would have been the moment where my body would have split into several pieces and melted in the floor. My mom just sat there quiet. Then she stood up, and held her arms out and asked, "What took so long?" It felt like a set up. I just knew the second I went in for a hug, she was going to swing at me, but it wasn't and she didn't.

Instead, she called my grandmother in as I wiped my face, sat her down and gave her the news. My grandmother just looked at me, smiled and said, "So you finally said it huh, you know grandmother always knew. I just don't want you to be in here touching that little boy." The little boy in question was my brother. I love him more than I can express, and the thought of touching him had never even crossed my mind. Just as beautiful as that moment was, it was ruined by the idea that now I had come out, I was now officially looped in with all the negative stereotypes that come along with being a gay man, including being a pedophile. I could barely speak of the comment and how ignorant it was, but I didn't have to. My mom looked at my grandmother and quickly redirected her ignorant comment. It felt like enough at the time, but it wasn't. It was one of those things that I sat with for years. The idea that my grandmother would ever think that I could ever hurt my little brother was beyond me, but the worst part of it all was that she didn't think that I would hurt him until she knew that I was gay.

I thought that the ignorance would stop there, but it didn't. At this point in my life, I had become old enough to realize that my grandparents had a drug dependency. They both had a healthy habit of doing cocaine. Every Friday, my brother and I would come home when we were staying with my grandparents and they would lock us in our room after a quick meal, usually a sandwich and some chips. This was unusual, considering that my grandfather loved to cook. They would turn the radio up to the max and get high. When I was younger, I knew that something was different about them on Fridays but I couldn't quite put my finger on it. The older I got and the more TV I watched, the easier it became for me to notice the correlation between their mood swings and the cocaine.

My grandfather wasn't a problem. He would usually get high and become really happy, or happier than he normally was. My grandmother, on the other hand, would get high, paranoid, and abusive. I remember waking up countless weekends and having to do miscellaneous things like having to scrub a bathroom with a toothbrush. I know that sounds like something straight out of a movie, but I assure you I didn't get any Box Office money for those chores and there was no trailer to retreat to once I was done. She would wake me up at two o'clock in the morning to do things like rearrange shoes or pick up trash in the yard, and because she was so high, nothing was ever good enough and I would get beat with whatever was close by.

Sometimes, that meant a shoe. Other times that meant a switch, and one time it was the crystal glass vase that sat in the kitchen.

The morning of that particular incident, she woke me up and asked me to wipe the hall mirror. At first, there were a couple hand prints, a little dust and some minor scratches, but after cleaning it three or four times, there was nothing there and she was still not satisfied. My emotions got the best of me and I just started to sob. Things had been happening like this every weekend for months and although it sounds selfish, I was upset because it was always me. It was never my little brother, nor did it happen to my little sister when she came over only me. The mirror was spotless and there was nothing else I could do, but she wanted it cleaner and when I refused to wipe it again. She picked up the vase and hit me in my forehead with it. I still have a small scar in the middle of my eyebrows from that day that even makeup can't cover. It reminds me of the person that drugs turned my grandmother into. She was always understanding and kind, yet mean, but only in the way that grandmothers can be. The cocaine turned her into a monster. Unrecognizable, It made me hate her.

For years I did, wishing that she would go away and get better like the celebrities on TV, or like the people in the movies, or like the one homeless man that I would see when I went to school who eventually got a job at the local subway. At first, I hated her, but as I got older, I began to hate the person that supplied her. They weren't just hurting my grandmother. They were hurting me in the process. I recall having a conversation with my mom about the way that I was being treated. I remember skating really around the topic of the actual drugs, due to the fact that my mom is very particular about her mother. Also, let's just say it wouldn't have gone over well for me to call my grandmother a coke-head in front of her. But for some reason, even though I didn't openly say it, my mom knew exactly what I was talking about. Since then, visits to my grandmother's house became less frequent, and over time I noticed that the drug use also became less frequent. I got my grandmother back, and while the time in between was nothing short of a nightmare, I was happy that it ended when it did. My grand father and I had always had a tight relationship and shared all the time we could talking about whatever even if it made n sense e at all. We would have rituals of watching wrestling every Friday night before the drugs started we'd sit in the kitchen and talk for 3 hrs while random people beat each other up for money and our entertainment. As he got older he would fill me in on the fact that it was all fake. He was my main man and I loved him like the world depended on it. Roosevelt was his name and he was clown. He was funny and always active my grandfather refused to sit down for more than a couple hours. He was a handy man and always needed a project which he usually asked for my help on. He could do no wrong and even when he did he always manned up to his mistakes immediately. When I found out he had cancer I blocked it out of my mind. Roosevelt was super-man, there was no way cancer was gonna take him out.

Six years later I got the call and I lost one of the best people in my life without being able to truly say goodbye .

Once we moved into my mom's house full-time I thought everything would be better. We had cable, all of our clothes were there, and we had really nice bunk beds. We were living the dream. Then I realized that the grass wasn't always greener on the other side. At my mom's house, my younger siblings had no responsibility. This meant no dishes, no sweeping, no mopping, no cleaning the bathroom. But what they did have was the liberty to mess everything up around me. I took offense to this, because if nothing else, my little brother had to at least wash the dishes after himself at my grandmother's house. Questioning my mother's authority however, was against the rules, and she made sure I was aware of that. It didn't matter how I felt, because as a child I had no feelings, and if I didn't like her rules I could leave. If I had a dollar for every time she said that to me, I probably wouldn't need to write this book.

If the chores weren't enough, my next obstacle was high school. I wanted to go to the local popularity contest that charades as the school known as Miami Northwestern. I thought I was a shoe-in considering that it was my mom's alma mater, but due to the fact that the school had a reputation for being in a highly homophobic area with lots of hate crimes against gay students, my mom quickly shut that idea down. I ended up going to Miami Senior High. I was upset about it at first, but at least I still got to wear the same colors. As it turns out, blue and gold were also the school colors of Northwestern, which at least made shopping for uniforms a lot more fun. In my head I just pretended that I was buying clothes to be a bull and not a stingaree. I thought that high school was supposed to be a turning point, but Miami Senior High became a breaking point, and I loved it.

CHAPTER 5

Goosebumps

The first day of high school was pretty stereotypical to say the least. I was scared and honestly had no clue what I was doing. The only knowledge I had of high school were the things I had seen on TV from Degrassi. I imagined my life would be a lot like Marco's. I would be fashionable, funny and get away with using snide and often uncomfortable remarks simply because I was gay, and eventually I would get one of the jocks on the football team to come out and be my boyfriend. I would be a cheerleader and we would be the "it" gay couple of the school.

However, this was not Degrassi. Miami high was not a predominantly white school; in fact, it was predominantly Hispanic. Most of my friends ended up being Spanish speaking Cuban kids and weird theater geeks. I remember wearing way too much cologne. As I walked down the halls and talked to different people, they all commented on how I smelled. I'll never forget it. My signature fragrance was "Sean John the One". It was a body oil concentrate that my mom had bought from some random guy at a local shop from a strip mall downtown, and I loved it. It was sweet and had a hint of musk so I didn't feel like I was wearing cologne. It was the closest thing I could get to perfume at that point, but I made peace with it.

I spent all day trying to figure myself out, where I would sit, who I would be friends with, who I would like, who I had already decided that I hated and so on. Yet, the one thing that I couldn't wait to do was figure out who my new theater teacher would be. It was my last period of the day and after sitting through Algebra, I needed a release, something creative. I had to walk up four flights of stairs and climb to what seemed like the top of the school. Tucked off in a little cubby on the top floor was the drama room. It had deep bay windows, a cute little stage and a small proscenium step set up. At the very back of the class, on the top of those steps, stood this slender and well dressed woman who reminded me of Ellen Degeneres. She had a nose ring and the most beautiful green eyes I had ever seen. She was wearing a navy blue pants suit and a white button down dress shirt that was open slightly to reveal the cleavage she didn't have. Her hair was cut in this curly style that was reminiscent of the 80s, tousled but not done. She wore this rose colored lipstick that was barely there but still made her lips stand out for some reason.

As I walked in the class, I realized that a lot of the people there already knew each other. Then I found out that it was a mixed grade class. There were seniors, juniors, sophomores and of course freshmen all wrapped into one class. Part of it excited me, while most of it scared me to bits. I sat down at the front of the steps in one of the stereotypical black theater chairs and just watched everyone come in. As the lady with the tousled hair came to the front of the classroom and said, "Hi, my name is Perdomo and I'll be your teacher for theater this year," the people behind me who had obviously been there before started to yell and scream for her like she had just won the superbowl. I felt like I was in good hands at this point. It wasn't my first time in theater and I knew that whenever the reaction was that epic, the teacher was usually as the bomb. And she was!

The first day we played theater games and got to know one another. I met a couple of different people that I gravitated to instantly. Cody was a 6'5" gentle giant. He was husky and had this very stereotypical anime cut. It seemed to always fall into place. The part was always on the left and his hair always seemed like it had just been cut. He wore these librarian style glasses that gave his face a cute mature vibe. Then, there was Cami. She was about 5'7" with this beautiful sandy brown hair that came all the way down to her butt. I was secretly envious of it the second I saw her. She was really skinny and had these doe eyes that could melt titanium. She didn't have an evil bone in her body, and to top it off, the girl was hilarious. Her best friend, Dani, was the complete opposite. She had this exotic look to her, very Rosario Dawson in my opinion. Her hair was deep brunette and had these natural curls that were to die for. Her eyes were big and round like a Bratz doll. She had this model-like figure that was curvy but thin. She was gorgeous and really quiet but funny once you got to know her. And how can I forget Jorge? He had this awesome smile with the big horse teeth and the military cut. His body was perfect, even though he was only about 5'8," he made everybody stop and stare. His arms were amazing. His butt was perfect and he knew how to dress himself, which was a rarity for most high school guys at the time. Lastly, there was Lysette. Think Regina George without the bitchiness. She had the perfect blonde hair, the perfect boyfriend, the perfect car, a great body and an awesome smile. Thank God for all of us, she actually had an awesome personality. We all quickly became friends. I met other people as the weeks dragged along. Carlos, the resident artist. Adil, the quiet nerd with Yu-Gi-Oh cards permanently attached to his hand. Irving, the man destined to be a star. Emily, Irving's best friend. And then there was James, the person that unknowingly would change my entire life.

A couple months had gone by and I had began to adjust. I knew my classrooms, I had started to make friends, the teachers were eating out of the palm of my hands, and I had started to be able to finesse my way around the administrative offices. Everything was golden and to be honest I realized that Miami High was probably the best choice for me. Being openly gay at that school didn't seem to bother anybody. I had dance for one of the periods in the middle of the day and often wore these short blue Hollister booty shorts in the middle of the gym because we didn't have a proper dance program. Of course, at first there were stares and snickers but eventually it became normal to everyone including me. I remember feeling like school was a home away from home. I remember being in love with the hallways, my friends, and even the crappy Papa John's pizza they would sell us at lunch. Because of my dance ability, I basically had to teach the class, and that was fine by me. The teacher who they hired was a yoga instructor: blonde, blue eyes and oblivious to actual dance techniques. Basically, I was guaranteed an A in exchange for coming up with routines to teach the class, which was completely fine by me.

Eventually, I was offered a chance to perform in the annual Hispanic heritage month showcase. It wasn't much because it was only the second year they had done it, which was surprising considering the percentage of Hispanic students at the school. It was in the library and I got a pass to skip class because of it, making it that much more fun to do. I had about three days to plan my performance. Although most people had seen me dance in the gym, this was different. I was going to be up close and some of these people had no idea who I was. After all, I was still a freshman. I spent the whole night before the performance trying to decide what I was going to wear. I had chosen to dance to "Hips Don't Lie" by Shakira ft Wyclef Jean. I decided to be minimal with my wardrobe and opted to wear some black ballet flats, my black tights, and a colorful traditional Cuban belt that Cami decided to lend me.

The next day I got to school made sure that everybody had my passes to be absent from class and got to the library right before the ceremony started. We had two different shows for the next two days, twice a day, which means that I got to be absent from classes four classes in a row. In hindsight, I realize that I would have much rather be in class so that I wouldn't have to catch up later. As a fourteen year old freshman, I was just happy to not have to do work. I didn't realize how big of a deal this was going to be. Although the performances were in the library, the social studies teachers were all instructed to bring their classes down to watch. That included one of the classes that I had been exempt from. Thank God I had no intent on skipping the performance. I started to sweat as I usually do right before a big performance. Considering that this was the first time I was ever going to really dance at this school, I felt nauseous and almost turned my performance into an Ashley Simpson 2004 jig.

I pulled myself together and right before they called my name I mustered up the strength to channel my inner belly dancing Columbian woman and gave it everything that I had. The crowd went crazy. I was out of breath and excited. The applause gave me a high like no other and I reveled in my emotions. I felt like a star and every single compliment that I got after just helped push the cause. I was on cloud nine and I wouldn't have it any other way.

After my first two performances, I had pretty much solidified what I was going to do. I tweaked the choreography and made the necessary adjustments to accommodate for space that I didn't have the day before. I went at it again the next day. The first show went off without a hitch, and the second show started off amazing, but right before the music was about to climax, I looked out into the crowd and spotted what appeared to be one of the most handsome men I had ever seen. He was 5'7," had this gorgeous mustache, a cute Jackson 5 and a Bill Cosby sweater. His smile lit up my entire chest and although most times during performances, I usually can't see anybody, I couldn't take my eyes off of him. We watched each other while I danced and I just remember telling myself that I had to find out who he was. I had to get to know this person. I had to make sure he became a part of my life.

As soon as this music was over, I was going to do just that. After everything had settled and the compliments calmed down, I looked around the crowd to see if I could spot the boy in the Cosby sweater. Finally, I saw him standing over near the checkout line talking to Cami and walked over. Even though I was only 5'10," I felt like I was towering over him. I tapped him on his shoulder and it was almost as if Cami knew exactly why I was there. She gave me that silent look of affirmation before she walked away. He had the biggest smile on his face which made me blush even harder than I had already started to. I asked him what his name was. He said, "James," and asked for mine. We exchanged pleasantries for about five minutes before I finally told him that I thought he was cute, and then quickly pulled back to ask him if he was gay. He laughed and responded yes, which made me happy. We exchanged numbers and for the first time, I felt like this was going somewhere. I'm not sure what it was about James. I don't know if it was his height or his cute sweaters or maybe even the way he went on and on about Disney, but he was different and I didn't have to have a full conversation to know that he was going to be a part of my life for quite some time and as scary as that was I knew I'd enjoy the idea.

That day I went home with his number in my pocket and contemplated about when I would actually use it. I kept thinking to myself: "What if he didn't answer? What if he gave me the wrong number? What if the conversation was just awful altogether?" It had never dawned on me that I should probably just call and by the time I mustered up the strength to do so, it was past my phone curfew. Even though it was Friday, my mom had strict rules on using the phone past nine o' clock. So, I played the waiting game. I barely slept thinking about what this conversation would be like. I played it out in my head over and over again. I thought about the cheesy questions I would ask and practiced laughing at all of his jokes. I tried to learn more about Disney so that I could be well-versed by the time we had our first real conversation.

Before I knew it, it was morning. I fell asleep with my iPod in my hand and woke up to the sound of Mulan singing "Reflection" and realized that today was the day. I waited until after breakfast and decided to call him around 10 o'clock that morning. The phone rang and my heart sank and once again my head filled itself with questions. What if he didn't like the things that I like? What if I was too much of a little kid? What if he thought that I was completely ignorant? Before I could answer any of those questions, the ringing stopped and he said, "Hello?" The conversation went on for what seemed to be hours. We both realized that we were watching the same Goosebumps marathon, and it quickly became the meat and potatoes of our conversation. We laughed at a lot of the situations and talked a lot about our personal interests. I found out that he really resonated with the story of the Little Mermaid and then revealed to him that I often felt a lot like Cinderella. That conversation was amazing. We realized that we lived across the street from one another, and quickly made plans to see each other the next day, which ultimately never happened due to my church obligations, but we didn't hang up the phone until my curfew at nine.

I had never talked to somebody for so long in my entire life. He made me feel empowered and special. I knew that everything I said was being retained and could be regurgitated if need be. He was listening. He was present, and that meant more to me than he could ever understand. I didn't want to lie to him. I wanted to be an open book. I wanted for him to understand me and allow me to understand him in return. That didn't take months of research. Before I knew it, I was feeling love for the first time. It was different than when I felt it with Kay. This was intense and it burned. I wanted to be present for every moment of it. Shortly after that first phone call, we spent every waking moment together. He would walk me to class and walk me home if he could, even though that was about an hour from our school. We made it there in about thirty minutes just because of the conversation. He would use his hall monitor passes to get me out of class and we would spend hours talking before theater. The only problem with this was the age gap. James was a senior and about to turn eighteen. I was fourteen about to turn fifteen and a freshman. As I'm sure you can guess, that rose a couple of questions for a lot of people. Yet, somehow we managed to make it work without worrying too much about the time and separation that was sure to come.

Eventually, our feelings became evident not just to the people around us but to both James and me. I'll never forget the first time he said, "I love you." We were on our way to the bus stop after a rehearsal and were deciding on whether we were going to walk or wait. We were holding hands and having a conversation about something completely unrelated to the subject of love when James abruptly let my hand go and froze. I stepped forward a couple more feet before I realized he wasn't following and turned around. He had this look on his face that creeped me out and made me smile at the same time. I finally mustered up the courage after about a minute of silence to ask him what he was thinking. He walked right over to me, grabbed both of my hands, looked me in my eyes and said, "I love you." I felt those words in a place that I had never felt them before. Sure, I had said it before and yes, I've had guys say it to me before this point, but this time I believed it. This time there was something different. This time I knew he meant it, and I was scared shitless, but I wasn't ready. I can still recall the look on his face when I pulled back and said, "I don't love you yet, but if you give me more time, I will." I could tell he was crushed, but he sucked up his pride, put a smile on and walked me home. By the end of the month, I was in love too, and he knew it. Everybody knew it.

CHAPTER 6

Almost Doesn't Count

The next few years of my life were very simple. It was me and James against the world. We went on dates. We talked. We explored each other sexually. He was my best friend, my lover and I just knew that I was going to have a fairy tale; that he was going to be the man that I married. I could talk to him about anything, and I did. He made himself available at all times for any subject no matter how silly I thought it was. He could do no wrong. I trusted every word that came out of his mouth, and worshiped the ground that he walked on. The best part was that I knew he felt the same for me. He took his time with me and trusted all of his fears, hardships and successes would be celebrated with and by me. Of course it's a far-fetched dream, but I felt like I had finally found my Jay-Z. All 5 foot 7 inches of him.

Everything was beautiful, except for one minor detail. My mom absolutely hated him, and it seemed like the closer that we got, the more she would come up with every excuse in the book for me not to see him. I would get grounded for the most minute things. Sometimes for six, seven, eight months at a time. Once I literally felt like I was grounded for a year, and I probably was. It would have been fine if I knew the punishments had been fair and not just to keep me away from him. As a typical teenager, all the punishments did was help me find different ways to get around them. James and I would seize every moment to sneak off together. Whenever my mom would leave for a night out on the town, I would run across the street to James' house and stay for hours, sitting in his front yard, talking with his little brother and sister, laughing with him and genuinely enjoying his time. I would skip tutoring on Saturdays and go to the movies with him.

I remember one weekend in particular, we went to go see a crappy knock off of Step Up. I think it was called Dance Flick. We went to an early showing, and there was nobody in the theater. We laughed for about thirty minutes at each other, and the rest of it is a blur. Let's just say neither one of us remembered a damn thing about that movie. It's always funny to me whenever I think about how movies were a big part of our relationship. Movies were like our happy place. We would watch them together over the phone, in person, talking about them, analyzing them, and breaking them down. It almost seemed to be therapeutic for the both of us. Some of our best moments happened while watching movies. James and I were sexual, but we had never had sex. In all four years, we talked about it, but it was never a priority.

One Saturday night in particular, when my mom made her usual run to the local adult function, James came over. All of my siblings were gone for the weekend and I was in the room watching Disney channel. I have no idea why we were both enthralled with the animated movie centered around a rat who could cook, but we were. For some reason, it sparked something in us. That night we had one of the deepest conversations of our relationship. In the midst of it all, James laid me down and we kissed for what seemed like forever. I was dizzy by the time he let me up for air, and in the moment, I felt like for the first time I was ready. Then, the phone rang. It was my mom just calling to check in on me, but my mother had a way about herself. For some reason, that call didn't seem like a check in. It almost felt like an "I know what you did last summer" moment, and to be honest, it freaked me out a little bit and killed the mood. James and I watched the movie until the end, and as bad as I knew I wanted to give myself to him, we ended another night with just a kiss. That was only one of the very many times that I faced almost certain death. My mom calls it being a daredevil. She says that me and my younger sister are the only two of the four of us that tests the waters knowing that if we got caught, she'd probably kill us.

James was worth it. My love for him was so strong that I was willing to do just about anything. I remember one of the last times he came over, my little brother was asleep. Once again, my sisters were gone and my mom and stepfather were out. It was lightly raining, and I called James to come over. For some reason, this night was set up differently. When James finally got to my house, he was wearing his signature look: a white T-shirt and these ratty blue basketball shorts with no underwear. Now I know that sounds like a setup, but it was honestly just the way that he walked around, and I loved those ratty blue basketball shorts. But James looked different that night. My little short husband-to-be looked like a man. His face was glowing, and his arms seemed bigger, and he didn't wear cologne, but that night he smelled so good.

Because my little brother was asleep, we went into my little sister's room and I was a floor person. I was literally the only person in the house that had a bed, but preferred to sleep on the floor. I grabbed a couple pillows and a blanket off of my bed, and James and I laid there. The light from the window created this movie like effect. The blinds created slits across our faces and bodies, and the sprinkling rain hitting the window made these water droplets look like dots of streaming lava hitting our skin. Something felt different about that night. We didn't speak, but we knew. The way that James straddled me was different. When I laid across his body, it was different. The heat was different. I remember him being on top of me, look me in my eyes in the darkness and somehow still managing to find a connection through the blackness and saying, "Are you ready?" I didn't respond with words. I just pushed my pelvis towards his and pulled him in for another stormy kiss.

Just as he started to undress and undress me, we saw the lights of car pulling up into my driveway. My heart stopped. James put his clothes back on so fast I thought he had super-powers. I ran to my room to look out of the window, and took a sigh of relief when I realized it was just my little sister's grandmother bringing her home early. My sign of relief quickly turned into anger. My first time with the love of my life was ruined. It was going to be so magical. I was about to taste the penis of a god, and this little bitch decides that she wants to come home early. Out of all the weekends, she had to choose this one. I was so upset, and James just thought the entire thing was hilarious. As soon as she got into the house, I forced her into the bathtub so that she wouldn't see James, and she made it extremely difficult. When I finally got her situated, James and I kissed once more. He left and I spent the rest of the night trying to figure out ways to murder my little sister in her sleep and not have my mom kill me in return.

Around one o'clock in the morning, I called James to talk about what had happened, and we both agreed that we were about to do something beautiful. Yet, somehow it never happened again. That heat never returned, and the moment was never as perfect. A couple months after that, things started to change. James started to feel insecure, and pushed me away. The closer I got to graduation, the more he seemed to distance himself. The pain of being forced out of that relationship was unlike anything I had ever experienced. It happened so gradually, and the lies started to take a toll on my head and my heart. I had no idea what had really changed. We had our minor disagreements, but I never thought that we would break up over them. I never thought that he would lie. I never thought that what I had with him would end because I thought he was perfect. I spent months trying to convince myself that it would all work out. We had countless conversations, and they all just seemed to lead in the same direction. It was over, and somehow he managed to still be a part of my life. We would still go on dates that weren't dates, share moments that weren't moments and talk about a love that was dwindling.

The day of my graduation from Miami High, I made sure that James had a ticket. Against my mother's will, he came and I almost cried through the entire service. I didn't realize it then, but as I look back and reflect on it now that was the day he said goodbye to me. That was the day that I lost the person that I loved more than I could ever imagine loving anybody on this entire bedrock we call earth. It broke me. James was one of the best parts of me. He taught me about patience, showed me that peace and love were a lot better than being angry all the time and reminded me that sometimes simply being kind was the best revenge. Although I had so much work to do, he was helping me through it, and I was in love with him for it. I hated him for leaving me to deal with myself. I hated him for forcing me to go out into the world without him. I hated him for taking the best part of me without warning, without proper cause, and without even trying, leaving me to fend for myself. That was never the plan. We were supposed to move to New York and struggle in the snow. He was supposed to be a starving artist who eventually wrote an amazing musical, and I was supposed to be the next Alvin Ailey without the tragic death. We were supposed to eat ramen noodles until our stomachs hurt and live in a crappy apartment that we made feel like home. He took that from me, and for that I think I'll always resent him. He took away my Cinderella story and gave me the impossible task of having to find someone to fill his shoes. The only problem is I didn't even know the size to start with.

CHAPTER 7

Hardwork My Ass

During high school, James wasn't my only concern. I focused a lot on my talents. Theater was going to be my way out. I was going to use the stage to get me out of Miami and my mom's house for good. I worked my ass off to make sure that I wouldn't have to ask her for a dime. I had scholarship money, and all I had to do was get in. I applied to the best of the best, NYU, the New York Film Academy and even AMDA. I was bound to get into one of them, and to my surprise I got into them all. There was no excuse for why I wouldn't be able to go. I had acquired at least five different scholarships with large lump sums of money so my mom wouldn't have the excuse of not wanting to pay to send me to school. All I had to do was accept an offer.

Because NYU was my first choice, I responded back so quickly that I think the postage still had spit on it. As soon as I got the letter, I called them immediately, and a woman in the registration office gave me the rundown. She politely explained to me that they would also be giving me a $10,000 talent scholarship because of my audition, and I got even more excited than I was before. Getting in was amazing, but getting in and having my talent be recognized enough to receive extra money was even better. That was, until she told me about the cost of living. Because they rented out apartment buildings instead of classic dorms, I had to pay $5000 up front. Although I had more than enough scholarship money, they had a policy that wouldn't allow me to use it to pay for my dorm. I had to pay it up front, and I had to pay it before I got there.

I was devastated. The look on my mom's face as I sat there on speakerphone had already given me my answer. I hung up the phone and immediately before we could even think of solutions, the first words out of my mom's mouth were, "You might as well find somewhere else to go because I don't have that kind of money and I'm not taking out a loan." I was crushed. I was angry, and I hated her. I did everything I was supposed to do. I got good grades. I graduated top 10% of my class, and I busted my ass to make sure that she wouldn't have to give me a dime. I got into the school of my dreams, and in the final hour, it was all thrown away because she refused to support me. I later on found out from my grandmother that my mom really had no intention and wasn't really happy about letting me go to New York. She was afraid I'd never come back, and if we're being honest, I probably never would have stepped foot back in Miami under my own influence. She took away my choice and ruined everything that I worked hard for. She didn't seem to care about the long hours that I put in and the amount that teachers poured themselves into me, or the time it took to get recommendation letter. None of that mattered to her. In her eyes, she had finally gotten a legitimate excuse to once again ruin my plans.

This time, I couldn't really blame her. Sure, it would have been easy to take out a loan, but as a single mom of four with my stepdad out of work at the time, I still had to be receptive to the fact that I wasn't an Orange County rich kid. I lived about ten blocks from the hood, and even though I had made it out, we weren't that far from it. That day, in those moments, I was reminded of where I came from. I was reminded of all the reasons why people never made it out. For the first time, I felt like I might become one of them. The next couple of days, I sat around the house moping, asking myself what my next move would be and rolling my eyes at my mother every chance I could. It was really tense, but for some reason she allowed me to throw my hissy fits without retaliation. I feel this is partly because I think she knew how much it hurt me to have to stay home. I only had one plan and New York was it.

Now, I had no James, no NYU, and no plan. I was sitting in the bed looking up design schools. I figured if I couldn't act, I would create. I had no real desire to become a designer, but it was the next best thing and the school I was looking at was in Miami but it did have a dorm room which was enough for me. However, in the moments leading up to me submitting my application, my mom got a call. Her godsister called to have a random conversation, and my mom filled her in on my situation. Her godsister explained to her that she went to Alabama State University, and she remembered the theater program being really good. I had no real information about Alabama, and I didn't do any research about the school. I just knew that Alabama was out of Florida and any place that wasn't Miami was worth a shot.

I submitted my application and woke up the next morning to an acceptance letter. This was all strange to me. I had to wait at least a month to hear back from NYU and all the other schools I had applied to, but Alabama State got back to me immediately. I was set to be at the campus the very next week, and although I still hadn't done any research, I was just happy to get the hell away from there. It seemed like the days started to go extremely fast after that. I would wake up, go to sleep and before I knew it, another day would pass. After what felt like thirty minutes, it was next week and we were loading up the rental to get me to Alabama. Before we left, we visited my grandparents house to drop my sibling's off. I remember the look on my grandfather's face. He was so proud of me, and my grandmother just sat in her chair and cried. My little sister was still too young to understand what was happening, but my brother who rarely shows emotion broke down for the first time.

My siblings and I are really close. They are like my babies. Even though I wanted so badly to get away, I wished I could take them with me. Seeing my brother cry like that reminded me of all the good times, the time he got his first pubic hair and ran into the room to show me. It was so microscopic, but he was so proud. Or the time that we snuck into the movies, jumped over the counter and snatched candy and drink only to find out that there was a door we could have walked through. I remember holding onto his innocence, and sniffing him one last time and still smelling my baby brother.

After our tears were shed, my mom, stepdad and I packed up the car and finally started to make the journey to Alabama. The trip that sometimes I wish I could have avoided. The ride wasn't long because my mom drives like a bat out of hell. The whole drive took eleven hours instead of thirteen, and she was proud of it. We made it to Alabama, and stayed the night with my mom's godsister's cousin. He was really cool, and I had two other play cousins that had come here for the same reason. As funny as it seemed, we all bonded instantly even though I had no idea who they were.

The next morning we all got up bright and early for student orientation. There were so many black people. Now don't get me wrong, I'm black and I love it, but growing up in Miami I had always been surrounded by a multitude of people from different backgrounds. Alabama State just looked like a sea of negros. My mom and I had no idea what an HBCU was, but because they used the word so frequently throughout that day, we finally mustered up the courage to ask. We quickly realized why there were so many black students on campus. I was slightly intimidated because all I could see where the faces of the types of men that were sure to taunt me for the next four years. My only relief was getting a dorm room that I didn't have to share with anyone. My mom made a big deal about me being gay and they assured her that I would be safe and that I wouldn't have to share a space with anybody. I have to admit that was one of the times where her overbearing personality was appreciated.

Before the orientation was over, while she packed up the car, her and my stepdad gave me a hug, and she placed $200 in my hand. Then she was on her way back to Miami. The second she left, I felt like a curse had been lifted. It was almost as if I had been living in a fairy tale and for the first time ever I could breathe fresh air. I almost wanted to break out in song. I wasted no time taking the necessary steps to become the person that I really wanted to be. My cousin was able to do some nice long braids and before I knew it, the transformation happened. I had already started to go by Hope by the end of my senior year so it made it easy for me to tell people that was my name. In fact, unless I had class with you, most people had no idea what my birth name actually was. On the first day of class, I remember wanting everybody. I put on this striped blue and gray T-shirt and a very short pair of DKNY jean booty shorts. I topped that off with a pair of gray Adidas, a blue headband and poorly done makeup. It took all the strength that I had to muster up the courage to leave my room that morning. I knew what I was in for, and I had to convince myself that I didn't care. My hair was cute, my makeup was what I perceived to be decent and my body was ridiculously in shape. I was going to make this campus my catwalk, and I did.

The second I left my room, all eyes were on me. If I could have recorded the faces of the boys in the dorm, you would swear you were looking at images from a horror movie. They were all disgusted, intrigued or just down-right scared. I had to remember that this was Alabama, and most of the people had never seen anybody openly express femininity in the way that I was. At that point in my life, I didn't identify as trans. I had no idea there was even a word for it, but I knew that I loved the way that I looked. I loved being able to express myself through my clothes and my hair and even my wretched makeup. I quickly became the talk of the campus. After about a week or so, I started to try and find my people: AKA the gays. I had noticed a couple of guys walking around campus who were obviously pitching for the same times as I was. However, I wasn't aware of was the need to appear masculine. A lot of the gay men in Alabama, especially on my campus, ignored me in the same way that the straight men did in efforts to fit in with the straight men. They did this in order to score a chance at having what we in the gay community call trade. Trade is essentially a down-lo or undercover straight man who plays around sexually with gay men. They are usually very masculine in appearance which makes them more desirable to feminine or flamboyant gay men. While the idea of that seemed nice, I was still getting over James and had no intention of giving myself to some confused football player. I did enjoy the attention that I got when nobody was looking though. Even though most of them were too afraid to admit it, they found me attractive. The late night knocks on my door for miscellaneous packs of noodles or random questions proved that to me.

Out of all of the new experiences that I had to adjust to, the one thing that never got easy was the walk into cafeteria. Our cafeteria was set up in an almost runway style scene. You had one long middle section that led you straight to the food, or if you weren't as bold, you could choose to take the sides and walk around. As uncomfortable at it made me, I always took that middle route. Most people would think it was because I enjoyed being seen. Some people would say it was because I liked the attention. But if I'm being completely honest, I did it because it was something I was afraid of. I was afraid to be stared at, and I was afraid of criticism. Every single time I walked into that cafe and had to walk that runway, I was forcing myself to be unafraid: to be in control of my feelings and remind myself that I had the ability to ignore the stares and judgement. It was my way of taking back that power. You can laugh, and make judgement, but you would never get me to not take that center runway. That was my moment, and for all of the years that I was there, no matter how many times people had seen my walk into the cafe, there was always a silent moment where everyone turned their heads and watched me and I enjoyed it every single time.

CHAPTER 8

His Name Was Quan (To Me)

While most people enjoy spending their breaks going home and visiting family, I spent the weeks leading up to every break trying to figure out who I was going to stay with. It wasn't that I hated my family, I just needed to get away and stay away. After spending my first spring break at home, I quickly realized that in such little time, so many things could change. All of my friends had either moved, gone to college, or gotten pregnant. This meant that when I went home, I spent most of the time alone or at the beach. The summer of my sophomore year was the hardest break of my life thus far. This was mostly because that was the semester that my mom figured out I had an affinity for hair weaves and let's just say she didn't agree. We had a huge argument which eventually led to us not speaking, and although she never said it, I knew that I couldn't go home.

I went to the counselor's office and had a sit down with a couple of the people there. I explained to them my situation and they tried to be as sympathetic as black, Bible-thumping Christians possibly could be. They ended up setting me up in temporary housing for the summer that was fairly close to campus. Everything was fine until I realized how lonely I was. I shared this huge house with about five other people from the school, who were apparently in similar situations. We all got along fine, the only difference was everyone else was working or had a significant other so usually I was left at home by myself.

In my solitude, I started to find self-pity which eventually led me to risky and pervy dating websites. I tried everything. If it a had a profile, you can bet I was on it. I went through what the average millennial would call a ho-phase. The problem with my ho-phase is that I couldn't get the ho part right. You see, to indulge in the ideal ho-phase, you must be willing to, in turn, be a ho. My definition of ho didn't seem to fit the mold. I was often seen as annoying and blocked. I think I got blocked so many times that at one point the websites actually shut my account down.

One night I decided to step out on a limb. I was going to be straight forward and put my money where my mouth was. I logged into one of my sites, scrolled for about fifteen minutes before I found an intriguing profile picture, and then politely slid into the DMs. My message was succinct and to the point. It read, "Hey, can I suck your dick." The second I sent that message, I regretted it and I felt like my heart stopped. I was hoping that he wouldn't respond, but to my surprise not only did he respond but it came almost instantly. He responded, "Sure."

In that moment, I knew I had to go through with it. I put on my big girl panties and sent him all of my info in hopes of getting this party started. About five minutes had gone by with no response, and then I heard the annoying little ding on my laptop. It appears that he had gone through my page and realized that I wasn't a female. Considering that I thought of myself as androgynous at the time, I didn't think it would take him that long, but I knew it would be a deal-breaker and part of me was excited about that. To my surprise, even after realizing that I was just a little gay boy with pretty braids, he still indulged in conversation with me. We talked about a number of different things for the next couple of weeks and he helped me get through summer. I didn't know much about him except for the fact that he had long dreads, caramel skin, and really great conversation skills. He made summer fly by, and by the time I moved back into my dorm, I knew that I at least wanted to meet him.

One day I texted him through the new app that we were now using and asked if he could bring me food. I had a long rehearsal and missed dinner so I was starving, and as a college kid I had two options, eat another pack of ramen or go to sleep hungry. I decided that the worst he could say was no, but he didn't and soon I was giving him my order for Taco Bell and setting up arrangements to meet him at the far end of the school next to a gas station. At the time, I didn't think about the fact that I was still meeting up with a potential stranger. It felt like I had known him for a while and through our constant conversation, he made me comfortable enough to take the chance.

When I finally got to our meeting spot and hopped in the car, it took me about thirty seconds to actually look at him. He drove this really cool black mustang. It was old, but the exterior was still sexy. I remember just sitting there grinning as he handed me the food. He didn't really say much so when he started to back the car up, I admit I started to think the worst. Once I was finally able to break myself out of my comatose state and formulate words, I asked him where we were going. He looked at me and gave me a smirk before saying he just wanted to find a place that wasn't so out in the open and told me to relax. We ended up finding this dead end street about two blocks away from the school. We sat there and talked until the sun came up and this eventually became a routine that happened just about every night for the next three years.

His name was Quan. He was 33, had two kids and one divorce under his belt. He was intelligent and funny and made me feel so uniquely comfortable. I trusted him instantly, and talked to him about everything, accomplishments, failures, successes, that one time I fell in the cafe, he became one of my best friends, but I wanted more and I had the feeling he did too. One night, we placed a bet. I can't remember exactly what the wager was, but I do remember knowing that I would win. My prize was a kiss. As a man of his word, he granted me that kiss. At first, he kind of just pecked my lips, and then looked at me and said, "What?" I giggled and responded that's not a kiss. I leaned in afterwards and had what I think was one of the best kisses so far.

Kissing led to touching. Touching led to licking and eventually we were having sex just as regularly as we were seeing each other. We would do it everywhere, in his car, outside that car, in hotels, behind buildings. He opened me up sexually and although he was not gay and never identified that way, he never excluded any part of my body. I feel like it was because he saw the woman in me way before I did. The way he touched me, talked to me and even the way he chose to respond to my life situations made me feel very feminine at all times. I could tell there was always a constant battle with him, at least the first year. It almost felt like he was always questioning himself whenever he would pull up to meet me. The sex was euphoric and we both pushed ourselves to do things that neither one of us had done before while still maintaining the friendship that made this all possible. I fell in love with him, and for the first time in a long time, I almost forgot James existed. Quan helped me cope through the homophobia I was experiencing at school and in everyday life. He reminded me that people were stupid, but it shouldn't dictate how I live. He taught me a couple of hard lessons about love and made sure that I knew it wasn't okay to just give up on people as a way to cope with heartache. He reminded me that I didn't have to be a classic beauty and that what I had was good enough. My broad shoulders, my thick legs, my particularly large hands and even my size ten feet were all good enough. Knowing that he felt that way made me happier than I had ever been.

We didn't have rules, but I knew that I couldn't go on a regular date with him. I knew that I would never meet the kids or play stepmom. I found out eventually that his name wasn't even Quan. It wasn't even short for something, it was just an alias. After a year and half of being personal and open with this person, I find out that he didn't even trust me with his real name. At first, I took it hard. I cut him off and refused to speak for about three weeks, but his persistence to be in my life made it hard for me to stay away. If nothing else he wanted to be my friend. He wanted me to be assured that our relationship was not based on sex. Although I knew that, it felt good to know that he wanted me to be sure of that.

I eventually found out his real name and realized that I didn't care to use it because I had no clue who that person was. I had fallen in love with Quan. I knew how he operated. I knew what he wanted. I knew how he felt about me which made it so much easier to forget the person that I didn't know in the first place. One of the best nights we've ever had took a lot of planning. We were driving around and ended up in a random town about an hour and a half outside of Montgomery. I remember telling him that we had to come back one day. He agreed and we set a date where we would go get a hotel and some snacks, watch TV while talking about the things that were happening with us both, and of course have sex. We had to make sure that we got an early start so instead of the usual twelve o' clock, he came and picked me up around nine. We got to the hotel and ran around to our room like kids. I told him about all of the things that I was doing in school, and for once he opened up to me about a couple of the things that he had on his plate. It was beautiful. For the first time, I fell asleep in his arms and didn't want to get up.

The ride back to Montgomery the next day didn't last long enough. I just remember telling myself that this is how it should be all the time. By the time I made it to my dorm room that morning, I remembered exactly why it couldn't be. I've held onto that memory ever since then. When the thought of transitioning first entered my mind, he was the first person to know. I talked to him about my new feelings and my thought process surrounding the change. He wasn't completely against it, but I could tell that he didn't feel it was necessary. This was one of the many reasons that I think I liked him so much. He liked me, not some overdone Instagram version of me; just the basics. At that time in my life, that's exactly what I needed. Even though it wasn't good for me and probably still isn't, he became a permanent fixture in my life.

CHAPTER 9

Mirrors Don't Lie

t was about 7 o'clock in the morning. I rolled out of bed, stretching a little, then threw on some basketball shorts and a T-shirt, grabbed my toothbrush and wash rag, gearing myself up to go prepare for class. Before I could open it, the mirror hanging on the back of my dorm room door stopped me dead in my tracks. I had a moment of silence with it. I stared at myself for what seemed like an eternity. I looked at my face with yesterday's makeup on it, my wigless head, and my ridiculously oversized clothes and had no idea who I was looking at. I had seen this person for the last three years. We had done this dance before, and usually I would smile and wave, then exit the room. This particular day I was frozen. I put my towel and my toothbrush down on my mattress, took my shirt off and dropped my shorts and just stood there looking. The voices of the guys outside slowly began to disappear as I got further into my own image. I couldn't move. All I could think about was wanting to run away, wanting to not have to dance this dance anymore. I cried in that spot uncontrollably for about thirty minutes. I allowed myself to sit there naked on the floor in immense pain tormented by the idea that I had lied to myself. I had been lying to myself due to the fear of losing the people I loved most. I had to ask myself the hard questions. I had to ask myself who I was living for and if I truly wanted the love of people who couldn't love me totally, unconditionally for the woman that I was about to become.

I still had no words for what I was feeling. I decided that I wasn't going to go to class that day. Instead, I grabbed my laptop and decided to search for natural hair tutorials. I have no idea why but in the midst of looking for ways to make my curls a little more defined, I stumbled upon a video of Janet Mock. This woman was so beautiful. She had this poofy, curly fro and this eloquence about her that made you want to listen to everything that she said. I watched about thirty videos back to back, each one more dynamic than the last. She was so poised and well-spoken, and then I found out something interesting: she was transgender. I realized in that moment, that the word I was searching for to describe me, the label to make myself feel at ease, was transgender. That's *exactly* what I was. Through watching Janet and doing my own research, I learned a lot about myself that day. I sent her the longest email, and was surprised to see that she responded. It was short and sweet, but encouraging. The next day I walked out of my room and was one person, Hope Giselle.

My first day as myself proved to be confusing and shocking for not only me, but the rest of the campus. While I'm sure most people figured that it was coming, not a lot of people figured that I would have the guts to do it while still trying to navigate being a student. At first, people didn't really notice me wearing bras and changing up the way that I executed my makeup. Eventually, I started to hear the rumors about how I had become an escort and how I was eventually going to go to Dubai and buy a body to resemble most of the video vixens. The next couple of months were hell, but they were so liberating. Having to explain to people that I had made the choice to embrace my transness wasn't easy. A lot of people didn't understand it, and most people had no intention of trying to.

Among that group was my mother. I decided to take a chance and visit home for winter break after two years. It shouldn't have come as a surprise, considering that there were pictures and plenty of informants stalking my social media. My mother knew all about the new me, but I guess there's something different about seeing it in person. Two days before Christmas, we had a huge fight. For the first time, I wanted nothing to do with her. I didn't want to see her, talk to her, or make amends. I was fine with pretending like she didn't exist. I didn't reach out to her and she did the same. She made it clear that I didn't have her support, and I made it clear that I didn't need it.

By the time I got back to Montgomery, the rest of the semester came down on me like a ton of bricks. I was a senior and all of my financial aid money had run out. All of my scholarships were exhausted and I had $5000 left to pay on my books or else graduation would be a distant dream. Due to our little silent treatment, there was no way I could ask my mom. I had to hustle and take whatever odd jobs I could get. This included cleaning houses for friends and even doing makeup and hair for the kids on campus. I started pulling in an income and soon enough my debt was paid. I made more than enough on a regular basis to support myself and my habits. Graduation was coming up and I had everything planned out. I was going to go to Texas and get my life together. I had met an amazing woman by the name of Kenya who selflessly offered me space in her home after only working for her for about a year. My self-proclaimed Montgomery parents Deidre and Jae, accepted my choice to move with hesitance, but let me go under the pretenses that they knew I would always have a place to come back to. I had been lucky that way. It always seemed that whenever I needed it, people were placed in my life at just the right times to make sure that I never went without.

The major turning point of my transition on campus was my relationship with Caleb. He was a new guy and came in as a freshmen during my senior year and he was also trans identified. Caleb was smart and funny. He had this quirk to him that I tended to gravitate to in men. Not to mention that he had a silent, but very predictable, active relationship with video games. Caleb was the only reason I passed math and got my name legally changed. He fronted most of our money, calmed me down when I got cold feet and was generally just an all around great brother to me. Caleb did the research I was too lazy to do, talked to the people I didn't make time to talk to, and even found the only doctor in Montgomery willing to perform HRT for us. A lot of the reason I am the woman I am is in large part to the push he gave me be more than just a social media figure. Caleb helped to me to be my authentic self on papers so that I had a means to fight with against bigoted professors and the ignorant administration. We made history as the first trans couple to ever walk in a coronation, and we did so with our heads held high in front of the entire campus, faculty, and staff. I've always been told that I was courageous, but the true courage is being my friend, and I commend Caleb for being able to do it. I thank all of my friends and chosen family for standing with me even in time of embarrassment, triumph, and failure. They never let me down or allowed me to feel like I was alone and though I can't pinpoint them all the amount of gratitude is unrelenting.

CHAPTER 10

Faith

Graduation day was supposed to be full of smiles, family and happiness. However, all I could think about the morning of graduation was how many things could go wrong. The fact that I didn't have a plan for where I was going to go afterwards and realizing that my grandparents wouldn't be able to come kept coming up in the back of my mind. I kept asking myself, "what if they say my name wrong? What if they use my dead name? What if my mom shows up and makes a scene? What if nobody shows up and when I walk across the stage it's absolutely silent?" I had a thousand negative thoughts running through my head and most of them stemmed from the fact that I had absolutely no idea what was going to happen and I was petrified. I got myself together in my dorm room earlier than usual and just sat there. I looked at my room still set up as if the semester wasn't over, as if my college career wasn't about to end in the next couple of hours. I remember wanting to cry so bad, and then telling myself that my makeup was entirely too beautiful. I made myself put on my shoes after about ten minutes. I grabbed my robe and headed down to venue.

As I walked past all of the families and students, I remembered how I pictured this day in my head. My little brother and my mom would make fun of me for deciding to wear heels while my grandmother and my grandfather would spend all of their time telling me how proud they were. My stepdad would spend most of his energy keeping my little sisters together. They would sit in their seats and when my name got called, they would be the loudest people you ever heard in your life. I would shake hands with all of the administration and we would end up at some cheesy buffet. Then, I'd lead them to go on some fantastic trip overseas.

Only problem is, that's not what happened. My best friends showed up along with one of my fans-turned-family who I lovingly call Mama Bear. We sat in the hot seats with our robes wrapped around us like a cult, and waited for my names to be called. I looked around the huge space and finally realized that while it would have been nice to have my family there, this wasn't for them. This was about me. This was about my work, and I was getting what I deserved. Nobody was able to take that away from me. In that moment, I was finally able to see past all of the distractions that I woke up with. I took one step after the other behind student after student and when I got up to the stage, I inhale deeply right before the dean of my college called my name. I had heard the words before, but hearing them that day were so much more fulfilling. I watched myself unfold and take in the moment. I gained a new sense of confidence. I hugged each and every one of my professors, took my picture, got my piece of paper and made my way back to my seat as a different person. Some people may not believe this, but after I got that degree, I saw things differently. I felt like I could do just about anything. I felt unstoppable. There wasn't too much I was going to be able to do about my mother at this point, but there was a lot that I could do about my circumstances.

Shortly after getting off of the stage, I had a conversation with Kenya about where I was going to go. Sensing that I didn't really have a plan, she offered me a place to stay until I got on my feet. I spent a couple more days in Montgomery, and then eventually caught a flight to Texas. I never would have thought that Texas would be home for me, but honestly without it, I'm not sure where I would have been today. Kenya opened up her family and her friends so that I could create a lane for myself. It took me about a year to acclimate to all that Texas had to offer. Everything seemed to be moving at warp speed, yet standing still at the same time. I picked up a job at a cosmetic counter which didn't last long. I quickly realized that the store manager had no intention on actually managing our store, it was falling apart quickly and she left us to sink alone. I needed my own space, and while the money I was making was okay, it was nowhere near enough to garner an apartment or a car. I hit the pavement and looked for everything in the cosmetic field. I finally struck gold when I got a callback from M.A.C Cosmetics. My starting pay was phenomenal, and this was basically my dream job. I had applied for this position in Montgomery, but was told that because I was transgender, I wouldn't be a good fit for the counter. The moment I accepted my offer, I imagined that look on that counter managers face in Montgomery and silently smiled to myself. I had made it.

In my first month of working I was able to buy a car and by month three, I had my own apartment. It was a nice studio with a bunch of space, lots of light, and just the right amount of hardwood and carpet. It was about thirty minutes from my job and I absolutely loved it. I never had company so the idea of furniture never really crossed my mind. I was donated a couch and a couple of bar stools. I eventually got a nice bed, a TV stand, and a really cool 55-inch smart TV. When I wasn't at work, I spent a lot of my days in bed watching Netflix and listening to music. I fell into this routine. I would go to work, come home, have dinner or not, fall asleep with the TV on and do it all over again. This happened for about a year. The same routine with the same faces and the same eventual feeling that I should be doing more, so I started to turn on my camera.

Facebook gave me an outlet. It created a space for me to vent, advocate and be plain silly. I don't know how, but I eventually amassed over 11,000 followers. People who just wanted to hear what I had to say no matter what it was about or when

I decided to get online. I came up with this concept called "Late Nights with Hope." It was a live show I would do every Wednesday where I would discuss issues that affected the LGBT community, myself, or just share funny stories. It became a huge part of my life. I would set up my room so that I had a permanent spot to film, and like clockwork every Wednesday, my loyal followers would tune in to watch me rant, rave, and even cry. I playfully called them my Hopefuls. Mostly because many of them keep me Hopeful. They watch my videos and think that they are the ones learning, but in all honesty, I'm the one being uplifted by them. They keep my ideas fresh and put me in check whenever I get out of line. They hold me accountable for my activism and the messages that I send out to the masses. They are a part of my little family and the support that they give help to make things a lot easier on the bad days.

My job started to become mundane and monotonous after a while. The little mistakes started to take a big toll and because it was my only source of income, I was forced into a position where I had to make a choice. I had been harassed and discriminated against and it always seemed as though there was nothing that anyone could do to help me. It always seemed as if everyone had an excuse for why it was okay for these things to happen to me. I would file a complaint, be pacified and then forgotten, but me being late or forgetting to sell a customer an eyeliner with her lipstick was never forgotten. I realized that I was becoming depressed and I didn't feel safe at work. One night I was followed to my car. Two men who didn't even work in my terminal decided to get off the bus and taunt me. Any other day this would have been fine, but I was working the closing shift and it was about 12:30. It wasn't dark, but there also wasn't enough light to make me feel safe. I heard them cackling behind me with the usual homophobic and transphobic slurs. I kept walking as fast as I could to my car. Thankfully I made it before they could get close enough to make contact with me. When I got into my car, clearly shaken up, they stopped in front of the window, kicked my hood and told me that they would get me later. It was moments like that which reminded me that I was different, that I was a woman but I was still trans. I had to mindful of where I was and who I surrounded myself with at all times. I had to be tactful in my approach with men and respectful in my conversations with cis women. I had rules and though they may have been ridiculous, I had to follow them to survive. I had to follow them to eat.

I was one discrepancy away from being fired. I had enough of my management team and my bills started to feel more like weights. I was unhappy with the way that my life was going, and although I know this sounds like a tagline for an ICDC commercial, it was my truth. I fell asleep as usual and completely forgot to set my alarm. I woke up to my phone vibrating furiously and to my surprise, it was my manager. I looked at the time on my phone and immediately broke down in tears. This was my last shot. I was supposed to open the store, and I blew it. I knew that there was no way I was going to be able to talk myself out of this one. They were going to fire me, and I had no idea how I would pay my bills if they did. My manager calmed me down, assured me everything would be okay and told me to come in once I got myself together.

I finally had the conversation and the verdict was up in the air. Because it was my final strike, my managers could do nothing to save me. We had to wait to hear back from the board, and in my year's time of being there, I had never seen anybody whose case went to the board come back with a job. I had to make a couple of decisions. I could chose to stay and allow them to figure out for me, or I could take a step out on faith. At the time, I was dating an amazing guy and once I told him the situation, he offered me a place to stay with him and his brother in LA. Although it all seemed crazy, it was better than potentially falling homeless in Texas. One more check, and I had a little over 1,200 dollars in my savings.

The next day, I went to work and the only thing on my mind was my next move. My customer service skills were sub-par and my attitude was like that of a menopausal Miranda Priseley. At around seven o'clock, I silently used the work computer and booked my one way ticket to LA, and by 8:30, I gave my boss my final notice. When the words came out of my mouth, I couldn't believe it. I felt like I was high. It felt like an outer body experience where I was watching myself make a mistake and had no control over being able to fix it. The logical thinker in me wanted to hit myself upside the head and scream, "what are you doing!? We can't just move to LA with some guy you've been dating for 6 months! Are you crazy?" But, the the artist in me stood firm on the crazy decision that I had just made. My manager gave me her reluctant approval and told me she wouldn't take me off of the schedule until I didn't show up which meant that I had two days to figure out if I was serious. Problem is, I also only had two days to pack.

The moments leading up to my flight time made me nauseous. I kept asking myself if I was sure. I kept running down my options and giving myself the what if treatment and all of my responses came back negative. I needed to make this move. I needed to change my scenery and get out of this funk. I needed to find myself and I wasn't going to be able to do that working customer service at the mac counter in the airport. I made my final decision, sold everything that I could and packed my life away into three suitcases, one box, a purse and a beach bag. I didn't tell many people about my move. I figured I didn't need judgement. By this time, my mother and I had made somewhat of amends, so the last thing I needed from her was a disapproving eye about my choices.

The day of the flight was the easiest. I made my way to the airport, checked my bags and called my boyfriend to let him know that it was all official. I was going to move to LA just like that. No plan, no real money, and not a clue about how the city worked. But I had a good feeling, and apparently that was all I needed at the time. I boarded my flight and slept all the way through, and touched down at about nine o' clock. I had been to LA before, but this time knowing that I wasn't leaving made the city seem so much bigger. Everything seemed permanent. Everybody seemed to be moving slower and the godlike quality of it all dissipated before me. All of the people that I would have normally admired from afar became targets for my silent ridicule. All of the men that I would have normally gawked at became little boys who no longer served my interest. Then, my ride came. I watched the buildings and the lights go by on the thirty minute drive and kept asking myself what I was doing. It was the first time in the entire ordeal that I questioned any of it. Part of me wanted to turn around and go back to Dallas, while the rest of me was just excited to be there. I was excited to have made such an irrational choice and petrified that I had actually followed through on it.

When I got to my boyfriend's house, I was greeted with a hug that I couldn't appreciate and a smile that would usually melt my heart. He gathered all of my bags and I made my way into the house. The next couple of days were filled with silent reflection and job hunting. I allowed myself to become immersed in the idea of becoming a well-versed advocate. I wanted to know everything there was to know about my community and the struggles that we were facing. I researched bills and laws and read articles every day. I applied to every center and health-resource management place that I could. I had amazing interviews and even better experiences, but that didn't stop me from being afraid: mostly about not being good enough. In my own little social media world, I was well-versed on my topics, but in LA, I was a small fish in a big pond. I felt the brunt of that reality really fast. I couldn't just come to this place and be mediocre. I had to set a tone. I had to build a brand and find a voice that was stronger than the one I had. I had to create an image that was more honest that the one I was presenting. I had to swim with the big fish and try to not get eaten, while at the same time be in love. It was all exciting and fresh, and I wanted to enjoy every moment of it.

I made it my priority to see something in myself that I hadn't seen in a long time. I meditated on my ideas and processed what it meant to be positive. I sat in my room for hours and wrote poetry and stories about my life as they presented themselves. I kept my thoughts bottled up, saving them only for the keypads of my phone and the innermost places of my mind. I abstained from social media, sex, and my tendency to require perfection. I opened up the door for self-exploration and challenged my thoughts on what it meant to be a woman, a black woman, a black trans woman in a society that tells you to be submissive, unheard, and judged by a particular set of standards. I forced myself to see the beauty in what was already gifted to me. I forced myself to find happiness in my flaws and I embraced them. I cut my hair. I changed the way I dressed. I even stopped wearing makeup for a while. In the process, I started to see the woman I'd been running from, the woman I kept hidden from everyone. She didn't need expensive weaves or heavy makeup and didn't feel the need to educate. She was happy with the simple things and enjoyed minimalistic living. She was the antithesis of the person that I had created, and I loved it because she was unfamiliar, unkempt and unruly. She made me feel like I was back in high school. The name Hope had no real meaning behind it until I grew older. At first it was just a disguise to hide from who I was pretending to be on social media, but it became so much more. It became a part of me. It became my armor. It became my shield, and it is who I am becoming while removing what's left of my disguise in the process.

"Being exceptional isn't revolutionary, it's lonely. It separates you from your community. Who are you, really, without community? I have been held up consistently as a token, as the "right" kind of trans woman (educated, able-bodied, attractive, articulate, heteronormative). It promotes the delusion that because I "made it," that level of success is easily accessible to all young trans women. Let's be clear: It is not."

— Janet Mock, Redefining Realness: My Path to Womanhood, Identity, Love & So Much More

ACKNOWLEDGMENTS

My Siblings - I love you all more than I can say. You're my number one inspirations and my best friends for life. Just know that I've always got your backs!

My Mother - You get on my nerves, but no one on this earth can replace you. Thank you for your constant growth and trying to see Hope past the son you had.

My Stepdad - You never judged me, even when I judged you. You accept who I am and you don't need to be convinced to do it! You love me and my brother like we're your own and I've always appreciated that! Thank you for being a man! In a situation where many would've been a bitch!

The Swains - Mom and Dad, I thank God for you two coming into that cupcake shop! You've loved me and helped me through some tough times and taught me how not to catch the musty, lol! You have always been honest with me and the door is always open to me like you said it would be. I cant thank you all enough, but I'm gonna try.

LaKenya - Ma if any one deserves a seat at the table when I make it, it's you! The sacrifices you made to make sure that I was ok in your time of crisis is a debt I'll never be able to pay back with money or time, but just know your investment in me is paying off.

Quan - I love you thank you for reminding me that the only words that have true power are the ones I give that power to.

James - You taught me that peace and love are what matter most when you're angry in these streets. You reminded me that being a kids isn't a bad thing and you showed me that no-one owes you anything. You are my first true love and I wouldn't take back a single smile or tear if I could.

Kay - You are a wonder and a true friend! Your love it unmatched and as my sister you have shown me more respect than most of my so called friends. I love you Kay and don't you let, time distance or space make you feel anything else.

Mallewi -You broke me in the best way. Thank you for the lessons, the growth, and the space to be exactly who I am, even when who I was wasn't so great.

Sky - You've been my HONEST friend , my personal assistant, alarm clock, and Tokyo to my Japan. Thank you for ALWAYS rooting for me even on the little victories. I love you so much, but you knew that!

Hopefuls- You all made this possible and kept me going through it all! You mean

the world to me and so does your support! I love you all!

God- THANK YOU